THE
PA SION
TRANSLATION

THE PASSIONATE LIFE BIBLE STUDY SERIES

12-LESSON STUDY GUIDE

THE BOOKS OF
JUDGES
and
RUTH

Light in the Darkness

BroadStreet
PUBLISHING

BroadStreet Publishing® Group, LLC
Savage, Minnesota, USA
BroadStreetPublishing.com

TPT: The Books of Judges and Ruth: 12-Lesson Bible Study Guide
Copyright © 2024 BroadStreet Publishing Group

9781424567621 (softcover)
9781424567638 (ebook)

Stock or custom editions of BroadStreet Publishing titles may be purchased in bulk for educational, business, ministry, fundraising, or sales promotional use. For information, please email info@broadstreetpublishing.com.

General editor: Brian Simmons
Managing editor: William D. Watkins
Writer: Matthew A. Boardwell

Cover and interior by Garborg Design Works | garborgdesign.com

Printed in China

24 25 26 27 28 5 4 3 2 1

Contents

From God's Heart to Yours

"God is love," says the apostle John, and "Everyone who loves is fathered by God and experiences an intimate knowledge of him" (1 John 4:7). The life of a Christ-follower is, at its core, a life of love—God's love of us, our love of him, and our love of others and ourselves because of God's love for us.

And this divine love is reliable, trustworthy, unconditional, other-centered, majestic, forgiving, redemptive, patient, kind, and more precious than anything else we can ever receive or give. It characterizes each person of the Trinity—Father, Son, and Holy Spirit—and so is as limitless as they are. They love one another with this eternal love, and they reach beyond themselves to us, created in their image with this love.

How do we know such incredible truths? Through the primary source of all else we know about the one God—his Word, the Bible. Of course, God reveals who he is through other sources as well, such as the natural world, miracles, our inner life, our relationships (especially with him), those who minister on his behalf, and those who proclaim him to us and others. But the fullest and most comprehensive revelation we have of God and from him is what he has given us in the thirty-nine books of the Hebrew Scriptures (the Old Testament) and the twenty-seven books of the Christian Scriptures (the New Testament). Together, these sixty-six books present a compelling and telling portrait of God and his dealings with us.

It is these Scriptures that *The Passionate Life Bible Study Series* is all about. Through these study guides, we—the editors and writers of this series—seek to provide you with a unique and welcoming opportunity to delve more deeply into God's precious Word, encountering there his loving heart for you and all the others he loves. God wants you to know him more deeply, to love him more devoutly, and to share his heart with others more frequently and freely. To accomplish this, we have based this study guide series on The Passion Translation of the Bible, which strives to "reintroduce the passion and fire of the Bible to the English reader. It doesn't merely convey the literal meaning of words. It expresses God's passion for people and his world by translating the original, life-changing message of God's Word for modern readers." It has been created to "kindle in you a burning desire to know the heart of God, while impacting the church for years to come."[1]

In each study guide, you will find an introduction to the Bible book it covers. There you will gain information about that Bible book's authorship, date of composition, first recipients, setting, purpose, central message, and key themes. Each lesson following the introduction will take a portion of that Bible book and walk you through it so you will learn its content better while experiencing and applying God's heart for your own life and encountering ways you can share his heart with others. Along the way, you will come across a number of features we have created that provide opportunities for more life application and growth in biblical understanding.

 ## Experience God's Heart

This feature focuses questions on personal application. It will help you live out God's Word and to bring the Bible into your world in fresh, exciting, and relevant ways.

 ## Share God's Heart

This feature will help you grow in your ability to share with other people what you learn and apply in a given lesson. It provides guidance on using the lesson to grow closer to others and to enrich your fellowship with others. It also points the way to enabling you to better listen to the stories of others so you can bridge the biblical story with their stories.

The Backstory

This feature provides ancient historical and cultural background that illuminates Bible passages and teachings. It deals with then-pertinent religious groups, communities, leaders, disputes, business trades, travel routes, customs, nations, political factions, ancient measurements and currency...in short, anything historical or cultural that will help you better understand what Scripture says and means.

 ## Word Wealth

This feature provides definitions for and other illuminating information about key terms, names, and concepts, and how different ancient languages have influenced the biblical text. It also provides insight into the different literary forms in the Bible, such as prophecy, poetry, narrative history, parables, and letters, and how knowing the form of a text can help you better interpret and apply it. Finally, this feature highlights the most significant passages in a Bible book. You may be encouraged to memorize these verses or keep them before you in some way so you can actively hide God's Word in your heart.

 ## Digging Deeper

This feature explains the theological significance of a text or the controversial issues that arise and mentions resources you can use to help you arrive at your own conclusions. Another way to dig deeper into the Word is by looking into the life of a biblical character or another person from church history, showing how that man or woman incarnated a biblical truth or passage. For instance, Jonathan Edwards was well known for his missions work among native American Indians and for his intellectual prowess in articulating the Christian faith, Florence Nightingale for the reforms she brought about in healthcare, Irenaeus for his fight against heresy, Billy Graham for his work in evangelism, Moses for the strength God gave him to lead the Hebrews and receive and communicate the law, and Deborah for her work as a judge in Israel. This feature introduces to you figures from the past who model what it looks like to experience God's heart and share his heart with others.

The Extra Mile

While The Passion Translation's notes are extensive, sometimes students of Scripture like to explore more on their own. In this feature, we provide you with opportunities to glean more information from a Bible dictionary, a Bible encyclopedia, a reliable Bible online tool, another ancient text, and the like. Here you will learn how you can go the extra mile on a Bible lesson. And not just in study either. Reflection, prayer, discussion, and applying a passage in new ways provide even more opportunities to go the extra mile. Here you will find questions to answer and applications to make that will require more time and energy from you—if and when you have them to give.

As you can see above, each of these features has a corresponding icon so you can quickly and easily identify them.

You will find other helps and guidance through the lessons of these study guides, including thoughtful questions, application suggestions, and spaces for you to record your own reflections, answers, and action steps. Of course, you can also write in your own journal, notebook, computer document, or other resource, but we have provided you with space for your convenience.

Also, each lesson will direct you toward the introductory material and numerous notes provided in The Passion Translation. There each Bible book contains a number of aids supplied to help you better grasp God's words and his incredible love, power, knowledge, plans, and so much more. We want you to get the most out of your Bible study, especially using it to draw you closer to the One who loves you most.

Finally, at the end of each lesson you'll find a section called "Talking It Out." This contains questions and exercises for application that you can share, answer, and apply with your spouse, a friend, a coworker, a Bible study group, or any other individuals or groups who would like to walk with you through this material. As Christians, we gather together to serve, study, worship, sing, evangelize, and a host of other activities. We grow together, not just on our own. This section will give you ample opportunities to engage others with some of the content of each lesson so you can work it out in community.

We offer all of this to support you in becoming an even more faithful and loving disciple of Jesus Christ. A disciple in the ancient world was a student of her teacher, a follower of his master. Students study, and followers follow. Jesus' disciples are to sit at his feet and listen and learn and then do what he tells them and shows them to do. We have created *The Passionate Life Bible Study Series* to help you do what a disciple of Jesus is called to do.

So go.

Read God's words.

Hear what he has to say in them and through them.

Meditate on them.

Hide them in your heart.

Display their truths in your life.

Share their truths with others.

Let them ignite Jesus' passion and light in all you say and do.

Use them to help you fulfill what Jesus called his disciples to do: "Now wherever you go, make disciples of all nations, baptizing them in the name of the Father, the Son, and the Holy Spirit. And teach them to faithfully follow all that I have commanded you. And never forget that I am with you every day, even to the completion of this age" (Matthew 28:19–20).

And through all of this, let Jesus' love nourish your heart and allow that love to overflow into your relationships with others (John 15:9–13). For it was for love that Jesus came, served, died, rose from the dead, and ascended into heaven. This love he gives us. And this love he wants us to pass along to others.

Why I Love the Books of Judges and Ruth

The times we live in are filled with challenges and moral choices. We seem to be living in an era of darkness that can only be lifted by the light of truth and grace. The two books, Judges and Ruth, are clearly a parallel universe to our present day. Here are some of the similarities:

- The people of God are facing mounting pressure to submit to the powers that be.
- The intercessory cries are rising for God to intervene.
- Enemies surround God's people, waiting for them to fall.
- But an answer is on the way—*deliverers*!

The Hebrew word *shophetim*, or "judges," can also be translated as "avengers" or "deliverers." One ancient translation renders it "saviors." The term describes the various men and women who distinguished themselves in Israel during the time period between the book of Joshua and the establishment of a kingdom in 1 Samuel. For four hundred years, Israel had no king or prophet to guide them. Instead, twelve consecutive judges led them. This era continued into the time of the book of Ruth.

But the Hebrew word for "judge" has little comparison to the Western concept of a judge, one who sits on the bench judging court cases argued by trained lawyers. The twelve judges have a parallel with the twelve apostles of Jesus. The book of Judges can be viewed as an apostolic manual for "last days" ministries. The judges were forerunners of the kingdom. God has promised that he will restore the era of deliverers (judges) in the last days to bring the church into complete victory (see Isaiah 1:26; Obadiah 21).

I like the books of Judges and Ruth (most likely written by the prophet Samuel) because they serve to *warn* the mind of the ease with which our human frailty and wandering ways can turn us from YAHWEH. Yet these books also serve to *warm* the heart by shining a bright revelation-light on our Savior's unspeakable compassion and long-suffering in the face of apostasy and disobedience.

Judges and Ruth show us that God uses imperfect people. He looks for those who are available, teachable, and obedient. Each of the judges had some form of weakness or handicap that would disqualify him or her in the eyes of some. But God looks on the heart and specifically chose each one to demonstrate his power flowing through human weakness. Yet while there was little to inspire us about their moral character, we do find a fount of faith flowing from their lives.

Although Judges exposes the many failures of God's people, it also reveals the faith of champions who chose to challenge the status quo, trusting in God's sovereign goodness and revealing his mighty power. The secret of their success was the anointing of the Holy Spirit (Judges 6:34) combined with an active faith in YAHWEH. In fact, four of the deliverers are mentioned in the "Hall of Faith" found in Hebrews 11:32. As the book reveals: "Through faith's power they conquered kingdoms and established true justice. . . . It was faith that shut the mouth of lions, put out the power of raging fire, and caused many to escape certain death by the sword. Although weak, their faith imparted power to make them strong!" (Hebrews 11:33–34).

By our Jewish friends, Judges is classified among the books of the Bible known as the "Former Prophets" (which also includes Joshua, Samuel, and Kings). This means that the content of Judges can be considered prophecy. This book prophesizes to the church today (1 Corinthians 10:11), instructing us of the ways of God through the voices of champion-deliverers who believed the Word of YAHWEH, confronted his people's enemies, and fought for their deliverance.

And who does not like a love story? The book of Ruth is endearing, engaging, and instructive on many levels. We see the covenant love Ruth demonstrated to her grieving mother-in-law Naomi. We see the incredible love God has for his people Israel (and for us today) in how he preserved them in days of darkness, despair, and famine. And we see the love Boaz had for Ruth, a gentile. He becomes a clear picture of our heavenly Boaz, Jesus Christ, our kinsman Redeemer.

How rich we are when we study these two books. They will challenge us to rise in greater faith to deliver others from darkness. And they will challenge us to remain filled with hope when gloom hangs over the land. I know you're going to love these books as I do. So enjoy your journey through Judges and Ruth!

Brian Simmons

General editor

LESSON 1

Downward Spiral

(Judges 1:1–3:6)

The American Western was a favorite film and television genre for decades. A courageous generation settling untamed territory captured the imagination of their settled descendants. The independence and freedom of that bygone society still holds appeal. At the same time, the frontier held challenges and dangers, such as shootouts, brothels, barfights, isolation, epidemics, vigilantism, and public hangings. Undeveloped society offers both sweeping possibilities and questionable morality. It wasn't called the Wild West for nothing.

The biblical book of Judges is the Wild West era of Israel's history. It is an era of settlers and frontier justice. It describes a time before ordered society, before fixed territories, before defined authority, when survival trumped stability. Consequently, this biblical book includes more brutality, sexual violence, religious chaos, lawlessness, and oppression than any other in Scripture.

In some ways, the harshness makes the lessons of Judges difficult to grasp. Modern readers have not experienced a society that is anything like Israelite society during that era. Furthermore, we don't want to. However, as current world conflicts show us, human depravity is unchanged. Society is fragile. Wild West living can resurface without much notice, especially when we reject the organizing principles of God's Word.

A God-Governed People

At the end of Joshua's conquest, the major cities and prominent kings of Canaan were conquered, but the task of settling the promised land was incomplete. While the Israelites had established their dominance over their new territory, there remained many strongholds to subdue. Although the tribal allotments had been clearly laid out, each of the twelve tribes had the task of driving out any remaining inhabitants in order to dwell peacefully in the land.

In only two generations, the people of Israel went from being chattel slaves to a nation of conquerors. They went from living in subservience to possessing and ruling their own land. In one generation, they went from camping in the wilderness living on miracle food from heaven to the responsibilities of maintaining, managing, and producing their own resources. The transition was swift and rough.

Moses brought Israel out of Egypt.

Joshua brought them into their new land.

Who would lead them forward?

During this steep learning curve, no capital city, no penal system, no human executive, no common infrastructure, no official currency, and no standing army existed. In such a situation, the reader could be forgiven for thinking there was no government.

However, God did not bring this people into the promised land only to abandon them there. In order for the Israelites to govern themselves, God gave them unique tools for ordering their society—tools they would need to fully embrace and utilize. They had the Torah. They had the priesthood. And they had the Lord himself.

The Torah (the Bible's first five books) was their chief asset. The Book of Law given through Moses included their ethnic and cultural history. It highlighted their exceptional place among the people of the world as God's chosen people. As such, they were required to live God's way, so the Torah also spelled out an ethical system of laws and obligations. The Law provided policies for virtually every aspect of life and restrictions to remind them of their uniqueness in the world, as well as penalties and remedies for violations.

God ordained the tribe of Levi, and especially its priestly class, to oversee the implementation of this new way of life. Their religious duties performed on behalf of the nation were meant to continually remind the people of God's character and requirements. Those duties included leading Israel in worship, proclaiming God's ways, dispensing his justice, and representing the people before God.

Hovering over these organizing resources, Israel had the favor of YAHWEH. If they loved and followed him, he would continue to care for them personally. He would fight for them in battle. He would prosper their work. He would bless their crops. He would expand their reign over the region. With their cooperation, he would exalt them above all the other nations. Simply looking at Israel would give the world an example of God's faithfulness, power, and love.

If they honored him, he would honor them.

If.

The biblical book of Judges is a collection of historical accounts from this transition period of Hebrew history. It is the narrative of a nation settling. Settling their land, of course, but also settling for less. Israel settled for less obedience than God required, less territory than God gave them, and less blessing than God desired for them.

Israel's Fail Reel

"Fail" video reels are another entertaining genre, at least for those with a slightly twisted sense of humor. Watching a tree surgeon miscalculate, a skier crash and burn, or a bride take a tumble is addictive. Why else would people tune in to watch a TV show featuring nothing but other people's home videos? Failure can be funny.

But Israel's string of failures in Judges 1 shows nothing

humorous. One tribe after another fell short of its potential. Compromising with their new neighbors, they settled for less land and heritage than God promised them.

- *What tribe took the lead in the continued settlement of Canaan (Judges 1:1–20)?*

- *Which tribe joined Judah in their conquest (vv. 3, 17)?*

- *What barbaric practice did they adopt from the Canaanites to demonstrate their dominance over their vanquished foes (vv. 5–7)?*

- *Take note of Judah's victories listed in this narrative (vv. 4, 8, 10, 11, 13, 17, 18) and the tribe's failures (v. 19). Overall, would you conclude that Judah was successful or unsuccessful in the settling of their allotment?*

- *How does the writer assess the tribe of Benjamin (v. 21)?*

- *What success did the tribes of Joseph (Manasseh and Ephraim) have in their efforts to secure their lands (vv. 22–26)? How did they fall short (vv. 27–29)?*

- *What about the tribes of Zebulun (v. 30), Asher (v. 31–32), Naphtali (v. 33), and Dan (v. 34)? What eventually happened to the land allotted to Dan (v. 35)?*

No matter how brutal the human summary of Israel's failures might be, it could never have the impact of God's own summary given through his divine messenger.

- *What historical events did the angel use to prove the faithfulness of God (2:1)?*

- *What specific God-given instructions had Israel failed to follow (2:2)? What would be the long-term consequences of their disobedience (v. 3)? How does this judgment compare to the warning God gave through Moses in Numbers 33:50–56?*

- *How did the people respond to this angelic pronouncement (Judges 2:4–5)? Did their response change God's mind?*

From this point on, the history of Israel is one of compromise, idolatry, and conflict with the surrounding peoples. The Israelites did not erase the idolatry and moral degradation of the Canaanites as God intended. Instead, the chosen people of God tolerated, accepted, and eventually adopted it. The downward spiral of the rest of the book of Judges bears this out.

Decaying Orbit

Every earth satellite faces a similar and lethal hazard, namely, a decaying orbit. Earth's gravity, tidal influences, and brushes with the outer atmosphere create drag on these objects. Without regular intervention from a vigilant ground crew, each revolution would bring them closer to fiery re-entry and destruction. Skilled software engineers program the corrections that counteract these influences and keep the satellite aloft. Israel's commitment to God was threatened by the same danger. Without regular seasons of repentance and renewal led by godly and humble leaders, decay and devastation were inevitable.

- *Judges 2:1–19 describes a decaying cultural-religious cycle of sin and deliverance. Read this passage and fill in the phases of Israel's decaying orbit.[2]*

Israel's Decaying Orbit Chart

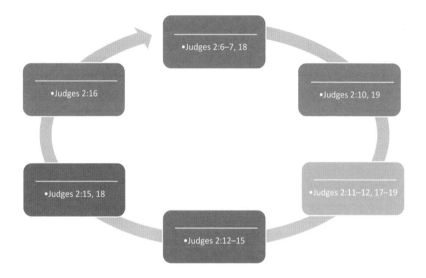

- *Compare Judges 1:1 to 2:8–9. What nationally important event is repeated? Does this parallel telling indicate that the book of Judges is a single narrative or a compilation of two accounts?*

- *Compare Judges 2:6–19 to Joshua 24:29–31. Notice how the same text can conclude one era and introduce the next. What phrase indicates that a new era was beginning?*

- *The writer of Judges describes a shocking type of ignorance for the people of God (Judges 2:10). What could lead to this dreadful level of ignorance?*

- *What two steps of rebellion did Israel participate in that enraged the Lord (vv. 12–13)?*

- *What did the Lord repeatedly use to punish his people's rebellion (vv. 14–15)? In their periods of waywardness, whom did they fight against in battle?*

- *How did the Lord respond to Israel's misery and oppression (vv. 16–18)? How does this compare to Exodus 3:7–10? What does this tell us about God's heart for his people?*

- *What phrase tells us that each successive cycle of sin took the nation lower into degradation and away from the Lord (Judges 2:19)?*

- *Ultimately, what did God decide to do about Israel's enemies living alongside them (2:20–23)? What was the Lord's purpose in this (2:22; 3:1–4)?*

- *What forbidden behaviors resulted from Israel's ongoing exposure to Canaanite neighbors and their culture (3:5–6)?*

Following the death of Joshua, Israel's failure to diligently complete their God-given mission led to other moral and spiritual compromises. Accommodating the Canaanites led to the tolerance of pagan customs and worship. This tolerance led to Israelite involvement in Canaanite idolatry and immorality.

To punish and correct his people, God allowed the surrounding nations to oppress Israel. This subjugation led to national misery that often (but not always) led the Israelites to cry out to YAHWEH for deliverance. Repeatedly, God displayed mercy toward his wayward people by sending supernaturally empowered men and women to rescue them and lead them back to the Lord. These heroes we call the judges.

Each deliverance was short-lived, though. The death of the judge began the cycle all over again. However, with each successive cycle, Israel's compromise sank to greater depths. The final chapters are so depraved that any film produced about this era would have to be NC-17-rated to do it justice. By the time this Bible book ends, the Israelites are so debased that their behavior is indistinguishable from that of Sodom and Gomorrah.

🕎 WORD WEALTH

Maybe we picture a judge as a distinguished legal scholar dressed in black robes and maybe even sporting a powdered wig, ruling over an orderly court proceeding to determine what justice requires. The judges of ancient Israel have little in common with that image apart from their devotion to judgment.

The Hebrew word *shaphat* (pronounced shaw-FAT) appears hundreds of times in Scripture. Its basic meaning is the act of judging or punishing. As in English, the corresponding title derives from this action. A judge judges.

Most of the time, this title refers to the Lord (see Psalm 75:7; 94:2; Isaiah 33:22). In Judges, *shaphat* occurs as a title only four times, all in 2:16–19. Most of the time, *shaphat* is what these leaders do rather than what they are.

Even so, we should not think of biblical judges presiding over court cases. The Bible describes only Deborah as doing that (4:4–5), though others may also have performed this function. Most of the judges were not even experts in the law of Moses. And some were less than just in their character and dealings.

How, then, did the judges of Judges judge? Their relationship to justice was far more judgment than judicial. Primarily, they were deliverers and avengers who rescued God's people and punished their adversaries. They wreaked justice on God's enemies. They brought judgment on Israel's oppressors.

Degeneration or Regeneration

Did Israel go through cycles of degeneration or cycles of regeneration? It depends on which part of Israelite history you observe. At times, as we shall see, they seemed determined to rush away from the ways of God. In the middle of those times, they were obviously on a downward spiral. But at other moments, as we shall also see, they rejected idolatry to return to God.

We can observe the pattern in our own lives. Seasons of stubbornness and repentance are familiar to all of us. The cycle of Judges is a reminder and a warning. Without regular times of discipline and correction, reflection, confession, and renewal, our focus drifts away from the Lord. Tolerance, compromise, and sin are ever crouching at the door (Genesis 4:6–7).

When we turn away from the Lord, may we be quick to return to him in repentance. By his grace and with the help of his Spirit, may we draw ever closer to him. Thanks be to God "for his mighty power has finally provided a way out through our Lord Jesus, the Anointed One!" (Romans 7:25).

EXPERIENCE GOD'S HEART

- *Romans 15:4 tells us, "Whatever was written beforehand is meant to instruct us in how to live. The Scriptures impart to us encouragement and inspiration so that we can live in hope and endure all things." Even the downward spiral of Judges is for our instruction, encouragement, and inspiration. Can you identify similar cycles of spiritual hunger and indifference in your own life? How would you describe your current status? Where would you place yourself on the cycles chart provided earlier in this lesson?*

- *We are tempted to stand in judgment over these ancient Israelites for failing at their task and turning away from the Lord, especially after he had done so much for them. But when we fail to live as God wants us to, what is our excuse? Ask yourself what makes you so prone to indifference, compromise, and sin, especially after Jesus Christ has done so much for you.*

♥ SHARE GOD'S HEART

- *When the tribes failed to take possession of the lands God gave them, the Lord confronted them with a hard angelic message of judgment. When would you say it is appropriate to deliver a difficult message to a sinful individual or group? Can you picture yourself delivering such a message?*

Repentance simply means to turn around. People going the wrong way need to change course. The further we go the wrong way, the longer it takes to correct. When we don't know the right way, we often choose the wrong one. A true friend will tell us when we need to turn around.

Talking It Out

Since Christians grow in community, not just in solitude, every "Talking It Out" section contains questions you may want to discuss with another person or in a group. Here are the exercises for this lesson.

1. After the angel told Israel that they would never possess the whole land, the people wept. Discuss whether this weeping was due to repentance or simply the disappointment of loss.

2. Judges is the story of a community, not of one individual. Israel shared the military failure. They shared the moral compromise. They shared the spiritual rebellion. Discuss how being part of a strong believing community can help a Christian stay on course. Discuss how a weak or compromised community can hinder an individual's faithfulness in convictions and conduct.

LESSON 2

The Noble and the Assassin

(Judges 3:7–31)

In literature and film, odd couples abound: Huckleberry Finn and Tom Sawyer; Sherlock Holmes and Dr. Watson; Rat and Mole in *The Wind in the Willows* by Kenneth Grahame; Legolas and Gimli from Tolkien's *The Lord of the Rings*; the classic comedians Laurel and Hardy. All these are fast friends whose stark differences enrich each relationship.

And, of course, there is *The Odd Couple* themselves, Oscar Madison and Felix Unger, two unlikely roommates from the Neil Simon play made into a 1960s film and 1970s television series. One cannot imagine two more different characters. One was fastidious, the other a slob. One was methodical, the other whimsical. One was stressed, the other laid back. One was miserly, the other generous. Every episode featured a humorous consequence of the two odd fellows forced to live together. Their side-by-side depiction exaggerated the characteristics of each.

Similarly, Israel's first two judges are a study in contrasts. In isolation from one another, we might miss these differences, but juxtaposed, the differences in pedigree, style, and tactics stand out between Cushan and Othniel.

The Noble

- *How long did Israel suffer under King Cushan? What two specific sins are called evil in the sight of YAHWEH? What did the Lord do to punish those sins (Judges 3:7–8)?*

- *Why did God send a deliverer to save the Israelites (vv. 9–11)? How did God indicate that Othniel was the chosen deliverer?*

- *What did God enable Othniel to do? What was the outcome of Othniel's courageous victory?*

- *Othniel is not a new Bible character. His biographical background is given in two virtually identical passages (Joshua 15:13–20; Judges 1:10–15). Who was Othniel's celebrated relative? How was he related? Which tribe did Othniel hail from? What feat of valor did he perform, and what was his reward for completing it?*

- *Compare the length of Israel's subjection under King Cushan-Rishathaim to the length of peace they experienced through the judgeship of Othniel. What does this indicate about the graciousness of God for his wayward people?*

"May you live in interesting times," goes the apocryphal Chinese pseudo-blessing. No one wishes to live in hard times. Easy, uninteresting, stable times are more suited for day-to-day happiness. But something terrible happens when a situation is too pleasant for too long. Courage fades, eternal principles are neglected, and life pursuits become trivial.

Hard times, on the other hand, demand strength of character. Hardship imposes perseverance and discipline. Difficulty reminds us of our mortality, frailty, and need. Adversity leads people to pray.

This is precisely what happened for Israel in their decaying orbit of sin. When the elders who knew Joshua and God's help in the conquest were alive, Israel thrived, they settled, and they enjoyed peace. Before long, however, placid living became complacent living. Comfort led to compromise.

Surrounded by their Baal-worshiping neighbors, Israel joined with them in marriage and religion. In easy times, when we are well-fed and secure, any old god will do. When we feel like we don't need God, it doesn't matter which god we don't need. So this divinely born, heaven-led, God-shepherded people forgot the Lord. It would take a severe thump on the head to get their attention. That thump came from King Cushan the Doubly Wicked.

We do not know much about King Cushan or his kingdom. We read that he was a ruler from Mesopotamia (literally, "between the rivers"). If the rivers are the Tigris and Euphrates, as we usually think of Mesopotamia, that description covers a lot of territory. Probably, this particular king ruled in the region adjacent to Israel known as Aram, north and east of Canaan in what would become modern Syria and Iraq.

The king's name is also a fascinating puzzle. The oldest English translations of Scripture give him the seriously long name Chushan-Rishathaim. (Imagine having to read that aloud in a Sunday school class.) Most versions of the Bible, including *The Passion Translation*, name him Cushan with the descriptive moniker Rishathaim tacked on.

Rishathaim means "doubly wicked." So, like Richard the Lionheart, Vlad the Impaler, and Edward the Confessor, this king would have been known as Cushan the Doubly Wicked. Scripture never mentions him again after Judges 3, so all we know about him is that this king was wicked. This was terrible for the Israelites under his thumb for eight years, so they cried out to Yahweh.

 DIGGING DEEPER

Suffering makes supplicants. People who know their need know enough to pray. The first times in Scripture that people call on the Lord are after eating from the forbidden tree, after banishment from the garden, and after the first murder. Following those moral disasters, as sin spread wherever there were sinners, it became obvious to people that they were in desperate need. "People began to worship YAHWEH and pray to him" (Genesis 4:26).

Whatever it takes to get us to call on the name of the Lord, it is a turning point. The Lord is not indifferent to our prayers or our sorrows. It was Israel's misery in Egypt and their outcry to God that moved his heart to rescue them (Exodus 3:7–10). It is because the Lord cares about us that we can cast our cares on him (1 Peter 5:7). The cry of helplessness always touches the heart of the divine Helper.

• *Read the following passages about calling on the Lord. Identify the individual caller, the need that motivated him or her to call, and their expectations of help.*

Scripture	Caller	Need	Expectation
Psalm 4:1			
Psalm 50:15			
Psalm 81:7			
Isaiah 55:6–7			
Jeremiah 29:11–14			
Jeremiah 33:3–9			
Jonah 2:1–6			
Luke 11:9–13			
Luke 18:1–8			
Romans 10:9–13			

0In response to Israel's cries, YAHWEH appointed Othniel as their deliverer. Othniel was a brave man, to be sure. When Israel's national hero Caleb called for a volunteer to overthrow the city of Dibir, Othniel did it. For his bravery, Othniel joined one of the most illustrious families in Israel. He received Caleb's daughter in marriage, a fine patch of land, and even the water supply to make it thrive.

Unlike every other major judge, brave Othniel seems to be a solid, faithful leader without any glaring character flaw. But the real secret to his success was the anointing of the Spirit of God.

To deliver Israel from Cushan-Rishathaim, the Spirit of God anointed him and empowered him for this task, and he accomplished it thoroughly. In a single sentence, without any additional details, this God-appointed, God-anointed leader overcame eight years of oppression and re-established peace.

Furthermore, Othniel was from the tribe of Judah, the strongest tribe of Israel. Their forefather Jacob saw the prominence of this tribe generations before when he declared to his children on his deathbed:

> O Judah, your brothers will praise you.
> You will conquer your foes in battle,
> And your father's sons will bow down before you.
> Judah, my son, you are like a young lion
> who has devoured its prey and departed.
> Like a lion, he crouches and lies down,
> and like a lioness—who dares to awaken him?
> The scepter of rulership will not be taken from Judah,
> nor the ruler's staff from his descendants,
> until the Shiloh comes and takes what is due him,
> for the obedience of nations belongs to him.
> (Genesis 49:8–10)

The tribe of Judah was destined to lead the nation. Throughout Judges, the prominence of Judah is clear. They were the first to tackle the continuing conquest of the land after Joshua (Judges 1:1–2). By far, they were the most successful at securing their allotted territory. More importantly, Jacob's prophecy indicated that one God-appointed, God-anointed leader would arise to rescue Israel and rule the nations. Eventually, this expected leader from Judah would be called Messiah.

As a flawless savior-leader from Judah, Othniel foreshadowed the coming Messiah. He judged Israel, but the Messiah would judge the nations. His leadership only lasted for a time, but the Messiah would rule forever.

The Assassin

- *Describe the repeated pattern that led to the need for another deliverer (Judges 3:12–14). What were the consequences of Israel's sin this time?*

- *What physical characteristic distinguished Ehud (vv. 15–18)? What tribe was he from?*

- *What task was he assigned by the Israelites that got him an audience with the king? Did he do this task alone? Describe the tool that Ehud had with him. Where was it hidden?*

- *What physical quality was notable about King Eglon?*

- *Was Ehud alone when he confronted the king (vv. 19–26)? What deception did he use?*

- *How did each man's physical characteristic contribute to this assassination? How did Ehud escape without triggering alarm throughout the palace staff?*

- *How did Ehud announce his leadership to the rest of Israel (vv. 27–30)? Where did Ehud and his followers take their stand to defeat the Moabites?*

- *How complete was Israel's victory over Moab? Compare again the length of oppression to the length of peace.*

What a contrast! Othniel is introduced with no distinguishing characteristics, but Ehud had a glaring one, namely, that he was left-handed. More precisely, the Hebrew text tells us his right hand was unusable. Whether Ehud was naturally left-handed or crippled in his right hand, we cannot be sure. Either way, this "abnormality" proved to be an asset.

Rather than coming from the chief of tribes, Ehud came from Benjamin, the least significant tribe in numbers and strength. The only mention of the Benjamites in Judges to this point was their complete failure to secure the land the Lord gave them. Certainly, some stellar individuals would come from Benjamin (King Saul, Mordecai and Esther, the apostle Paul, to name a few), but the book of Judges paints a tragic picture of the tribe as a whole.

Valiant Othniel confronted King Cushan-Rishathaim in open warfare, but the assassin Ehud killed Israel's oppressor by deviousness and cunning. Under false pretenses, he secured a private audience with King Eglon, who had grown fat taking tributes from Israel. Because Ehud had already been in the palace without incident, the king unwisely trusted him to return. Ehud had perfectly placed his homemade dagger in his unexpected dominant hand, strapped secretly to the unexpected right side. Eglon, eager to hear this secret, stood to receive an unexpected "message" from the Lord and exposed his enormous belly for the death stroke. In went the sword, out came the excrement, and down went the king.

Ehud did not even have to fight his way out of the palace. He locked the door from the inside and secretly escaped through a balcony or porch. The palace staff did not want to disturb the king. It smelled like he was probably relieving himself. Finally, after they waited an awkwardly long time for him to finish his business, they intruded only to find him dead. By that time, Ehud was far away, stealing his way home.

As the word went out that King Eglon was dead, his soldiers stationed in Israel scurried back toward Moab. Ehud led Israel's fighting men to block all the crossing points of the Jordan River. When the Moabites tried to cross over, they were killed. Through Ehud the assassin, the tables were turned so completely that Israel dominated Moab after that.

- *What judge is briefly mentioned after Ehud's era (v. 31)?*
  What weird victory did he win? What do you think it
  means that his name isn't even an Israelite name?

🅗 WORD WEALTH

The God-appointed deliverers Othniel and Ehud were human models of YAHWEH's own character. This is especially true when we look carefully at the title he gives them.

The Hebrew word *yasa* (yaw-sha) is a common root for the cluster of words about salvation. It is used over two hundred times and often translated as "save," "salvation," "safe," or "deliver" (for example, see Genesis 45:5–7; Exodus 15:2; Esther 4:14; Isaiah 19:20; 25:9). In combination with YAHWEH, the name of God, *yasa* forms the names Joshua and even Jesus, names meaning "the Lord saves."

It is this word that the people quoted to Jesus when he entered Jerusalem on a donkey (Mark 11:8–10). The enthusiastic crowd spread out their cloaks and palm branches on the road to welcome him, crying, "Hosanna! Blessed is he who comes in the name of the Lord!" (v. 9 NIV). They were repeating Psalm 118:25–26, which predicted Messiah Jesus coming to the temple. *Hosanna* means, "O save!"

As with the first two judges, sometimes *yasa* is rendered as the title "deliverer" or "savior." Most often, it is a title reserved for YAHWEH himself (2 Samuel 22:3; Isaiah 43:3, 11; 45:15, 21; 49:26; 60:16; 63:8; Jeremiah 14:8; Hosea 13:4; Micah 7:7). However, in a handful of cases like these, the Lord raises up someone to represent him, someone who will deliver his people for him. Even then, the Lord is the source of this salvation. Even then, the Lord can say, "I, only I, am YAHWEH, and there is no Savior-God but me" (Isaiah 43:11).

Our True Deliverer

Whatever their differences, Othniel and Ehud had this in common: God graciously raised them up to deliver his people. Experiencing the consequences of their own disobedience and rebellion, Israel was suffering. Each time the Lord cared about their troubles enough to send a judge to rescue them. They did not deserve one. They did not earn this favor. These were pure acts of mercy on the Lord's part.

The Lord always saves out of his mercy. We are all lost and weighed down by our own sin due to our own attitudes and decisions. On our own, we would continue in the wrong direction, in trouble, and away from the Lord. However, YAHWEH sees us in this dangerous situation, and he cares. Even before we know we are lost, he takes steps to save us. He sent his own Son, Messiah Jesus, to seek and save the lost (Luke 19:10).

We do not earn his rescue. We cannot. He does not look for the healthy to heal, the clean to cleanse, or the righteous to make holy. He directs his love toward sinners (Mark 2:17). The Good Shepherd loves lost sheep (Isaiah 53:6). Simply put, there is no other kind of human being for God to love.

It is in God's nature to love. He doesn't have to work at it. It is what he is like. How grateful we should be for that! It is God's boundless love that motivates him to save (Titus 3:3–7). He wants us to be safe, delivered from danger. He wants us to be whole, delivered from immaturity and weakness. He wants us to be forgiven, delivered from sin. He wants us to be reconciled to him, delivered from alienation. Because of his nature, he wants these things infinitely more than we do. He wants to save us more than we want to be saved.

YAHWEH delivers. YAHWEH *wants* to deliver. YAHWEH *is* our Deliverer.

❤ EXPERIENCE GOD'S HEART

It would be tragic to marvel at the way the Lord saved Israel without seeing that the Lord wants to save you. We need to see how lost we are without his help. We need to see what danger we are in without his rescue. We need to see what Jesus did to save us from our sin and separation from God. Then we need to call out to him in repentance and faith. "Everyone who calls on the Lord's name will experience new life" (Romans 10:13).

- *Read Titus 3:3–7 carefully. Consider what motivates and does not motivate God to save us. Thank God for his mercy and this eternity-changing truth.*

❤ SHARE GOD'S HEART

- *How does it help to know that the Lord is eager to save? Think of someone you know who is in spiritual trouble and needs to experience his salvation. Sincerely pray for their deliverance.*

- *Why do you think it is difficult for some people to call out to the Lord for a rescue? Think about what assurances or experiences you could share with them that might overcome this reluctance.*

Talking It Out

1. How can hardship and suffering produce spiritual growth and renewal (Romans 5:3–4; James 1:2–3)? Talk about the people you admire who have gone through severe trials. What role did their suffering play in forming their character?

2. Discuss how the Lord can use both the direct (Othniel) and the devious (Ehud) to accomplish his purposes. Share examples from your own life or from someone you know.

LESSON 3

A Pair of Heroines

(Judges 4–5)

Americans tuning into NBC news on November 11, 1975, heard Tom Brokaw sternly announce, "A freighter carrying a crew of twenty-nine disappeared on Lake Superior during a severe storm last night and, so far, no survivors have been found. The freighter, the *Edmund Fitzgerald*, was transporting iron ore when it ran into high winds and 25-foot waves."[3]

This brief report captured the facts but none of the emotion or description of the maritime disaster. A dispassionate news bulletin can never do that, but a song can. When Gordon Lightfoot recorded the "Wreck of the *Edmund Fitzgerald*"[4] in 1976, with its haunting melody and on-board perspective, listeners gained a deeper understanding of the event itself.

Similarly, the judgeship of Deborah is summed up in two chapters: the first a narration and the second a song. One captures the facts, the other the feelings. Together, they give us a clearer picture of her era of leadership.

- *Place the historical description in Judges 4:1–3 on Israel's Decaying Orbit Chart from lesson 1.*

- *What people group, king, and general were involved in God's discipline of the Israelites (4:2)? What specific component of their war machine is mentioned as the key to their military superiority (v. 3)?*

When Israel first came into the promised land, Hazor was a powerful city. Its king, Jabin I, led a confederacy of Canaanites to war against the encroaching Israelites who were under Joshua's leadership (Joshua 11:1–11). That battle resulted in the complete destruction of the city and the death of its king. More than a century had passed since then, and the city of Hazor was rebuilt. The surviving Canaanites rallied there and adapted the best of contemporary military technology (Joshua 17:16; Judges 1:19). A new king, Jabin II, took the helm, and under his leadership, Hazor became a powerhouse once more, right in the heart of Israel's territory. This was the clear and deadly result of Israel's failure to fully obey the Lord's command to take possession of the land.

- *Who was the judge of Israel during this era (Judges 4:4–5)? What is unusual and maybe surprising about this leader? How did the writer describe her responsibilities as a leader?*

- *Whom did Deborah commission to fight against General Sisera (v. 6)? What tribes of Israel would participate in the fight? Where would the battle take place (v. 7)? Who made the battle plan?*

- *Under what terms did Barak agree to wage this battle (vv. 8–10)? Why do you think he demanded this? Does this seem courageous or cowardly? What were the predicted consequences of this condition?*

The Bible is clear about this point: Barak was a hero of faith (1 Samuel 12:11; Hebrews 11:32). Therefore, we must be cautious of our first impression of him in this interaction. He was not cowardly. He was a courageous leader of warriors. He would take a limited number of soldiers with limited weaponry against an intimidating enemy with top-notch gear. He was not faithless. This valiant plan directed by YAHWEH took great faith to carry out.

Perhaps Barak believed that with Judge Deborah's involvement, he could muster more troops. Maybe he had more confidence in her spiritual rapport with the Lord than in his own. Certainly, he already had faith in her instructions. We do not know his motivations, but we do know he adamantly wanted her presence.

Deborah was agreeable but disappointed with this demand of Barak. Because God had already declared the victory, her presence at the battle was unnecessary. She did go to battle with Barak, lending additional strength to this warrior. However, she promised him that if a woman was pivotal for initiating the battle, then a woman would be pivotal for concluding it.

- *Who informed General Sisera that the Israelites were preparing for war (Judges 4:11–16)?*

- *Who was the most important warrior on Israel's side that day (vv. 14–15)?*

- *How did the Canaanite war machine fare against the poorly equipped Israelite fighters on foot?*

Valiant Barak commanded his warriors. Steady Deborah was present to initiate, to witness the battle, and to pray. But the clear winner of this conflict was YAHWEH. He drew the enemy in to battle (v. 7). He gave them into Israel's hands (vv. 7, 14). He went ahead of the Israelite troops into battle (v. 14). He routed Sisera's army (v. 15). With the Lord's help, the victory was total. No chariots could stand against him. No human soldiers could survive against him.

- *Why do you think Sisera jumped out of his mighty iron-fitted chariot (vv. 15, 17)? Why would he abandon a highly coveted weapon of war in the middle of the battle?*

- *Where did he go for refuge (vv. 17–20)? Why was he confident that he would be safe there?*

- *What did Jael do to reassure him and cajole him to sleep? How did Jael fulfill Deborah's promise that a woman would be the ultimate hero in this war (vv. 18–22)?*

- *How did this military defeat contribute to Israel's completion of the conquest against the Canaanites of Hazor (vv. 23–24)?*

As Deborah prophesied, a woman achieved this victory, and an unlikely woman at that. Jael was Heber the Kenite's wife. We know from 4:11–12 that Heber's camp had a great vantage point on the battlefield and that he was an informer to Sisera. The general expected to find asylum there, not an assailant. At first, Jael's hospitality convinced him that he was safe. With the sedative of exhaustion and warm milk, Sisera fell fast asleep...forever. Jael's devious plan never entered Sisera's head. Until the spike did.

The description of the battle in Judges 4:14–15 is concise, to say the least. The two armies fought; Israel won. The narrative only zooms in on the scene of Sisera's death. But many of the details surrounding this battle are filled in by the celebration song that Deborah and Barak sang together after the victory.

A Story Song

The bards of ancient Celtic societies sang lengthy songs recalling battles and heroic deeds. In Greece, rhapsodes performed jokes, myths, and historical epics through long, elaborate songs. Skalds kept Scandinavian history alive through the generations. Some of these European traditions are familiar to us, but history in song was a worldwide phenomenon. Judges 5 is one such song from ancient Israel.

- *Compare the prose of Judges 4 to the poetry of Judges 5. Notice the details that are unique to one passage or the other to complete the historical account.*

Detail	Narrative – Judges 4	Song – Judges 5
What was daily life like under the oppressive rule of King Jabin II? How safe was living in the land and traveling along the roads? What weapons did Israel have to resist tyranny?	4:1–3	5:6–8
Who initiated the resistance? Which tribes participated in the battle?	4:4–13	5:2, 9–18, 23
What natural events displayed the Lord's engagement in this conflict? What phrases indicated that angelic fighters were also involved?	4:6, 9, 14–15, 23	5:4–5, 20, 23
How did the iron-fitted chariots become a detriment to the Canaanite army?	4:14–16	5:19–22
What women are portrayed in the celebration song? Whose grief is portrayed?	4:17–22	5:24–30
What were the long-term results of this pivotal day? What kind of people were blessed by Deborah in the aftermath of the battle?	4:23–24	5:31

Some Trust in Horses

Joshua shook his head in disbelief at these leaders. Their parents and grandparents had been slaves together in Egypt, but God showed his power and set them free. He brought them out of bondage and through the sea on dry ground.

They did not even have to look back that far to see the Lord's abilities. He had revealed himself to their own generation. Only a few years before, they camped on the banks of the Jordan at flood stage, but God showed his power and stopped the river's flow for them to cross (Joshua 3–4). Together they had witnessed God's power in victory over every enemy they faced. Jericho collapsed (Joshua 6). The Southern alliance was conquered (Joshua 10). The Canaanite confederacy was destroyed (Joshua 11). All with the divine help of the omniscient God.

But now, when the allotments of the land were made, the Israelites complained, "All the Canaanites who live in the plain have chariots with iron-rimmed wheels" (17:16). After all their experience, they trembled at modern war machinery (vv. 15–18). They overlooked their overcoming God.

Joshua would have none of it. "There are indeed many people in your tribes, and for that reason, you are very powerful...You will conquer all the Canaanites even though they not only have iron chariots but also are a strong people" (vv. 17–18).

These same iron-reinforced chariots were the boast of Captain Sisera in his battle against Israel in Judges 4–5. They were intimidating armaments, indeed. They could roll over enemies and repel Israel's meager hand weapons. Still, those chariots turned out to be no match for the Lord. Just like Pharaoh's army at the Red Sea (Exodus 14:25), YAHWEH thwarted these chariots with water. No matter how mighty the war wagon is, it is no match for a torrent from the Lord.

Maybe these two chariot incidents were the inspiration for the psalmist when he wrote:

I know Yᴀʜᴡᴇʜ gives me all that I ask for
and brings victory to his anointed king.
My deliverance cry will be heard in his holy heaven.
By his mighty hand miracles will manifest
through his saving strength.
Some find their strength in their weapons and wisdom,
but my miracle-deliverance can never be won by men.
Our boast is in Yᴀʜᴡᴇʜ our God,
who makes us strong and gives us victory!
Our enemies will not prevail; they will only collapse and
perish in defeat while we will rise up, full of courage.
(Psalm 20:6–8)

The people of Israel had to learn, repeatedly, that the Lord would fight for them *if* they would trust in him alone. Great armies or warriors do not intimidate the God who made everything from nothing and sustains all of creation with his powerful word. On the other hand, if the Israelites trusted in themselves, their military prowess, or false gods, the Lord would just as readily fight against them. He will fight for the faithful, but he will not defend the indefensible.

Christians can be just as confident in the Lord's ability to fight for and defend them. When we are afraid or reluctant, we overlook our overcoming God. He still stretches out his hand to fight on behalf of his faithful people (Acts 4:30). Our battles are spiritual, of course. Therefore, we fight differently than Israel did (2 Corinthians 10:3–5). Our enemy is just as determined to destroy us (John 10:10; 1 Peter 5:8–9), but we are well able to overcome him with the help of the Lord (Romans 8:31–37; 16:20; James 4:7; Revelation 12:10–11).

Leading Women

Most of the leaders in the Bible are men. This fact makes the mention of female leaders a curiosity, but we seem more surprised by it than the biblical authors. For example, Deborah's leadership is understated, delivered in a matter-of-fact manner. She is simply introduced as a prophet, the wife of Lappidoth, and the leader of Israel. This pattern plays out with almost every female leader in Scripture.

- *Read the following passages and find the women mentioned and their role in leading God's people. Match the individual with her leadership role(s). Take note of how naturally the authors write about their positions.*

_____ Anna (Luke 2:36–38)
_____ Apphia (Philemon 1:2)
_____ Deborah (Judges 4:4–5)
_____ Esther (Esther 4:13–16)
_____ Euodia and Syntyche (Philippians 4:2–3)
_____ Huldah (2 Kings 22:13–17)
_____ Junia[5] (Romans 16:7)
_____ Miriam (Romans 16:6)
_____ Mary, Joanna, Susanna (Luke 8:1–3)
_____ Miriam (Exodus 15:20)
_____ Nympha (Colossians 4:15)
_____ Philip's daughters (Acts 21:8–9)
_____ Phoebe (Romans 16:1)
_____ Priscilla (Romans 16:3–4)
_____ Tryphena, Tryphosa, and Persis (Romans 16:12)

A. Apostle
B. Apostolic coworker
C. Christ's companions
D. Deacon(ess)
E. Host of a local church
F. Judge
G. Prophetess
H. Royal deliverer

❤ EXPERIENCE GOD'S HEART

- *Some Christians experience the Lord best through song. Something about the music or the emotion of the poetry expresses their soul better than prose. What do you think about that?*

- *What makes worship through song so powerful?*

- *What do singing worshipers contribute to the life of the church? Are there any dangers to this?*

- *Like Barak, you may be tempted to think someone else is better qualified to face a spiritual challenge. Like Barak, you might miss out on the reward God wants for you. How do you know when God has given a task specifically to you? Why might you be eager or reluctant to do it?*

♥ SHARE GOD'S HEART

- *When someone is resistant to the gospel, we often assume there is some intellectual or tactical problem. If only we explained it more clearly. If only we were more winsome. If only we told the story in a more entertaining way. Does it occur to us that the obstacles to faith could be spiritual? Think about a resistant person you hope will believe Jesus' good news. Pray to our overcoming God for them.*

- *Think of a surprising spiritual victory from your past. Look for the opportunity to share that experience with someone else who needs to hear it.*

Talking It Out

1. Jesus promised his disciples that "In this unbelieving world you will experience trouble and sorrows, but you must be courageous, for I have conquered the world!" (John 16:33). Discuss the spiritual battles you are fighting lately. What obstructs or opposes your spiritual progress? What temptations are hard to overcome? How do you persevere when you feel attacked? How does it help to know that Jesus overcomes?

2. We are not likely to be intimidated by iron-clad chariots these days, but we can still be afraid. What technologies, natural abilities, organizations, or situations intimidate you? Talk together about the weapons with which we fight spiritual battles (2 Corinthians 10:3–5; Ephesians 6:10–18). How would these help you overcome?

LESSON 4

The Reluctant Warrior

(Judges 6)

Across the developed world, young men are struggling with a failure to launch. At the stage where they could be tackling the adventure of life, gaining independence, and establishing their own homes, instead they withdraw from adult responsibility into a developmental loop where they "never grow up." The Western world refers to this as Peter Pan Syndrome; in Japan, it is *hikikomori*, which translates to English as "pulling inward." For a variety of cultural and personal reasons, more than a quarter of young men simply lack the resolve to take life's next step.[6]

What keeps young men from doing what they need to do? Some suggest this demotivation stems from an excessive focus on safety and security. Accustomed to the comfortable provision and emotional affirmation of overprotective parents, they are paralyzed by a fear of failure or danger.

Sometimes insecurity idles them. They doubt they are equipped for the challenges they face or that they are the best person suited for a job or obligation. Without a track record of responsibilities well performed, they are uncertain that they can perform at all.

Still others are grounded by hopelessness about the outcome of their effort. A sacrifice of time, effort, and pleasure could result in disappointment. What if they put in the effort only to end up back where they started? Why bother?

Whether the cause is fear, insecurity, or hopelessness, millions are reluctant to initiate life. As a result, they are shielding themselves from pain, but more poignantly, they are missing some of life's greatest joys: freedom, family, and vocation.

Our Reluctant Warrior

Gideon, Israel's next judge and one of its most well-known, seemed to be stifled by a lethargic cocktail of these demotivators. Having grown up during the peace of Deborah, Gideon knew comfort and security. But in its cycle of sin, Israel faced a new threat from its neighbors, and the situation had become bleak. YAHWEH found Gideon floundering in fear, insecurity, and hopelessness, and Gideon reluctantly found the Lord.

- *What initiated the next wave of enemy oppression (Judges 6:1)? How long did it last? How did Israel try to escape the oppression of Midian (v. 2)?*

- *How did this nomadic group, as well as others, dominate Israel (vv. 3–5)?*

- *What good result came of all this raiding (v. 6)? How did God initially answer Israel's cry for help (vv. 7–10)?*

- *God's messenger found Gideon in an unlikely place. What was he doing? Why was he doing it there (v. 11)?*

- *How did he greet Gideon (v. 12)? What is strange about this greeting? Does Gideon agree with this estimation (v. 13)?*

• *What task did* Y*AHWEH* *have for Gideon (vv. 14–16)? Why was Gideon reluctant to carry it out?*

• *Was Gideon confident that this message was from God (vv. 17–18)? What evidence did the Lord give to show Gideon that he wasn't imagining things (vv. 19–21)?*

• *Did this settle Gideon's nerves at first (vv. 22–24)? What words did assure him? What did Gideon name his new altar?*

Ordinarily, harvesters did the threshing out in the open, where a breeze could catch the chaff and blow it away. Gideon hid his work inside a winepress so the raiders wouldn't notice that he had something worth stealing. The Israelites all lived this way, hiding and skulking, but still they couldn't keep what they had. Their misery led them to call on the Lord and "everyone who calls on the name of the LORD will be saved" (Joel 2:32 NIV).

So in that winepress, the Lord met Gideon to announce his saving plans. Gideon's responses weren't promising. He disagreed with almost every word spoken to him, from the greeting to the assignment. It wasn't until fire miraculously consumed the meal Gideon offered his guest that he realized what power he was dealing with. Only then did he begin to cooperate.

Objecting to the Lord

Because we can't see the whole picture, the Lord's plans don't always make sense to us. At times, his plans seem downright unreasonable, so we drag our feet or protest. Understandably then, Gideon is not the only Bible hero to object to the Lord's instructions. Several of his followers quarreled or negotiated with God, but each in turn submitted to his will. Every mortal must conclude: "The Lord YAHWEH, the Commander of Angel Armies, has an amazing strategy, and who can thwart him?" (Isaiah 14:27).

- *Look up the following passages. Make a note of the objector, the objection, and the outcome. What can we learn from the way the faithful have expressed their doubts directly to the Lord?*

	Objector	Objection	Outcome
Genesis 18:20–33			
Exodus 3:4–15; 4:1–17			
Jonah 3:8–4:11			
Matthew 3:13–15			
John 11:38–44			
Matthew 16:21–25			
John 13:4–17			
Acts 9:8–19			

An Inside Job

- *What initial challenge did YAHWEH give to Gideon (Judges 6:25–32)? What problem was he confronting? Was Gideon bold or timid in carrying out these instructions? How do you know?*

- *How did the townsfolk respond to the destruction of their idols? How did Gideon's father defend him? Was he correct? How did this threat resolve?*

The first verses of the Gideon account don't indicate the evil that Israel did to provoke the Lord, but now we know. The people had plunged into idolatry again. Their towns had enormous shrines built to the Canaanite deities of Baal and Asherah. What tragic irony! Baal and Asherah were deities of fertility and fruitfulness. Worshiping them was supposed to lead to abundance and prosperity. The crops and herds would flourish, the barns would be full, and the people would be wealthy.

Instead, as a direct result of their religious unfaithfulness to the Lord, Israel was sacked by their enemies over and over again.

Routing the human enemy had to start by rooting out these spiritual enemies. As Bible scholar Barry G. Webb states, "There could be no having the Lord as their deliverer while they had Baal as their god."[7]

Jesus taught his followers this same principle. Before we turn to address the issues *around* us, we must confront the sin *in* us. Otherwise, it is like trying to help someone remove a speck from their eye when you can't even see clearly because of the beam sticking out of your own eye (Matthew 7:1–5). What a ridiculous image that is! The speck is a problem, of course, and that other person might need help with it, but our efforts to confront sin should start with our own.

In the dark of night, Gideon struck his first blow for deliverance. These shrines became a pile of rubble and kindling. The locals didn't like it, and even Gideon's father was steeped in this idolatry. But when the neighbors came for Gideon's blood, his dad made the best case for Baal: an all-powerful god can take care of himself. If Baal wants Gideon dead, he can kill him.

When Gideon lived on, this arrangement proved the impotence of their false gods. The people even gave Gideon a new name that mocked Baal. Of course, this was only one victory at one shrine in one town, but it was a turning point. It demonstrated that Gideon was willing to confront God's enemies and that God would protect him when he did, so he turned to face the Midianites.

Mercy for Doubters

- *What people groups crossed the Jordan to invade and occupy Israel (Judges 6:33–35)? What four tribes did Gideon muster to confront them?*

- *How many troops rallied to Gideon when he blew the trumpet, and how many left him (7:3)?*

A massive army of Israelites came when Gideon called. Apparently, he wasn't the only warrior fed up with the raiding of these human locusts. This tremendous affirmation from his own countrymen might have been enough to steel the spine of other military leaders. What about the reluctant warrior Gideon?

- *Was Gideon confident enough now to initiate an uprising (6:36–40)? What two opposite signs did he request from God to reaffirm his promises? Why do you think Gideon needed so much reassurance?*

This episode of Gideon's life is one of the most familiar. Sometimes Christians use it as an example of how we can seek the Lord's direction for a particular decision. We hear that Gideon showed us how to "lay out a fleece" before the Lord in faith. We are assured that a miraculous sign like this will provide the answer we need.

Certainly, God can and might lead us with supernatural signs, but this was no model for faith. Actually, it was the opposite. Gideon needed God to affirm and reaffirm the direction he had already given and already confirmed. Wasn't it enough that God had miraculously consumed the meal Gideon offered him? Wasn't it enough that he had protected Gideon from his own vengeful townsfolk? Wasn't it enough that tens of thousands of soldiers were ready to fight at his side to throw off their persecutors? No. It wasn't enough for Gideon. He needed yet more reassurance from God. And, once again, our gracious God showed mercy to this reluctant warrior.

"There's no way I'm going to believe this unless I personally see the wounds of the nails in his hands, touch them with my finger, and put my hand into the wound of his side where he was pierced!" (John 20:25). So said Thomas, one of Jesus' apostles and a key leader in the earliest Christian missions.

Others had seen Jesus alive. They were initially skeptical, too, when the women announced his resurrection (Luke 24:11–12). But after Jesus showed up in person, they were convinced by the evidence he showed to them: his hands, his side, and his ability to eat food (vv. 36–45). He settled their doubts with his own presence.

But Thomas wasn't there. He didn't get to see these proofs. It wasn't obvious to him that the others weren't just being carried away by their collective wishful thinking. He would have to see for himself. So Jesus appeared just for Thomas. The Lord had mercy for the doubter.

He didn't leave them to flounder just because they had doubts. When the disciples called out to him in the storm afraid for their lives (Mark 4:35–41). When Peter was overwhelmed by the waves he was miraculously walking on (Matthew 14:28–33). When the father brought his helpless demon-possessed son to Jesus (Mark 9:20–27). When the disciples didn't know where their food would come from (Luke 12:22–31). In every case, Jesus personally proved his power to protect, guide, heal, and provide.

Jesus always hoped for faith, but doubt didn't unsettle him. While doubt isn't noble, it is normal. All of us experience doubt. At some point, all of us have doubted the Lord's character, his Word, or his promises. All of us can relate to those who doubt.

That's why Scripture urges his followers to show godly mercy to doubters (Jude 20–23).

The Lord performed the impossible signs Gideon demanded to give him the confidence to step forward in faith. As we will see in our next lesson, even this wouldn't be the last time the Lord showed this kind of mercy to this chronic doubter.

🐾 EXPERIENCE GOD'S HEART

- *Have you ever been reluctant to begin a God-given task? How did you know he was prompting it? Did fear, insecurity, or hopelessness play a part in your reluctance?*

- *Did you overcome the issue you had? If so, how? If not, why?*

- *Some Christians are not self-reflective at all, so they critique everyone else without giving attention to their own issues. Others fixate so much on their own shortcomings that they never feel competent to help others address sin. Which tendency do you have? Do you understand how either is a mistake? When do you feel it is appropriate to confront the evils we see around us?*

 SHARE GOD'S HEART

- *Imagine facing doubt and uncertainty without the Lord to help you through it. Think about what it must be like to rely only on yourself for protection, guidance, healing, and provision. Now pray for people you know who are in that situation.*

- *Tell someone else a story about some reassurance our merciful Lord gave you to overcome your doubts so you could take the next step of faith.*

Talking It Out

1. Doubt is a common experience, even for Christians who trust the Lord. Share with the group what serious doubts have tested your faith. Talk about what restores your faith when you doubt.

2. Look up and discuss some of these verses about showing mercy to each other: Micah 6:8; Zechariah 7:8–10; Luke 6:32–36; Romans 12:6–16; James 2:12–13; Jude 1:20–25. What is the basis for our mercy toward one another? What role does mercy play in maintaining a healthy community of believers?

LESSON 5

Rise and Fall of the Underdog

(Judges 7–8)

Sixty thousand. That was the recruiting target for all branches of the United States military in 2022. Out of 330 million people, the military needed only sixty thousand of them to enlist. However, despite expensive and creative advertising campaigns, record-high signing bonuses, and increased outreach efforts, the year ended with a 25 percent shortfall in new enlistments.[8] The reasons for the shortfall are debated, but a gap of this magnitude presents a serious long-term problem.[9]

Why do armies want large numbers? Simply put, they want to win wars. Generally, the side with the best weapons, the most resources, and the largest troop numbers wins. The underdog loses.

The history of Israel is uniformly different than that. Without lifting a finger, they plundered mighty Egypt (Exodus 3:20–22; 12:33–36). As barely freed slaves, they defeated the Amalekites (17:8–13). They conquered the ancient fortress city of Jericho by walking around it (Joshua 6:12–21). As Barak's battle with Sisera's forces demonstrated, even the best armaments wielded by an intimidating army cannot conquer the Lord (Judges 4:14–16).

In our last lesson, we noted that Gideon lacked confidence, needing regular reassurance from the Lord. And the Lord graciously gave him every confirmation he asked for. Now this same reassuring God was going to test Gideon's faith in radical new ways.

- *How many soldiers rallied to Gideon's cause (Judges 7:1–3)? What did the Lord think of this incredible recruitment success? Why did he want smaller numbers? How did they pare down the numbers? How many remained at the end of verse 3?*

- *Is it surprising that so many soldiers were afraid? Explain your answer.*

- *After two-thirds of the men peeled off to go home, was the Lord satisfied with the numbers (vv. 4–8)? What method did Gideon use to sort them? After the final selection of soldiers, what percentage of the original force was still with Gideon? (Hint: for the math-challenged, the answer rhymes with fess fan fun fercent.)*

Much speculation has been offered about why the Lord chose these three hundred over all the others. Some scholars suggest that the men who lapped like dogs were more eager or reckless. That the others were too wary for the Lord to use. This speculation misses the point. The Lord wanted a teeny-tiny underdog force to press the attack so Israel would know who won the victory. This is why he chose the smallest group for the biggest job. The Lord wanted underdogs.

Besides, the law of Moses actually *commanded* limiting the number of warriors (Deuteronomy 20:1–9).

- *Compare Moses' instructions about going to war (Deuteronomy 20:1–9) with the instructions given to the initial army of Gideon. What filter did Gideon use that was prescribed in the law?*

- *What additional exemptions from military service did Moses stipulate but Gideon did not use here?*

- *How did Gideon's easily counted army compare to the camp of the Midianites and Amalekites (Judges 7:8–12)? What two illustrations did the writer use to show the difficulty of numbering Israel's enemies? What estimate was later made about the size of their army (8:10)?*

- *What further encouragement did the Lord provide to Gideon before the battle (7:10–11, 13–15)? What were the enemies dreaming and talking about when Gideon sneaked into camp? What had they concluded about the battle ahead of them? How did Gideon respond to what he overheard?*

Psychological warfare was already underway. The Lord had already frightened the enemy with unsettling premonitions. After all, what armed warrior wouldn't be afraid of a reckless loaf of bread? When Gideon overheard the Midianites, he realized that God had already defeated the Midianites and their allies. God, who had persuaded him that he could win this conflict, had also persuaded his enemies that they would lose it.

So Gideon worshiped the Lord. He bowed down in reverence to God's sovereignty and love. We don't know if there was any other content to Gideon's worship. We don't know whether he prayed or sang or simply fell silent. We don't know what this worship entailed, only that his response to these defeated enemies was to acknowledge the Lord. Then he left the discouraged horde to encourage his underdog army.

- *What weapons did Gideon's forces carry into battle (7:16–18)? How were they to use these "weapons"?*

- *Describe the effect that this strategy had on the enemy (vv. 19–25). Why do you think it was effective? Whose swords wiped out the enemy?*

- *What role did the rest of Israel play in the battle's aftermath? Where have we seen this tactic before (3:27–30)?*

- *Gideon was from the tribe of Manasseh, and some of his fellow tribesmen were among the three hundred. What tribe resented that they weren't included in that strategic surprise (8:1–3)? How did Gideon calm their anger?*

Operation Desert Thorns

For most Sunday school students, the story of Gideon ends after the battle of jars and torches. If only Gideon's story ended there. He had confronted and condemned idolatry. The underdogs won a total victory. Israel's territory was completely liberated. Israel had driven Midian away never to rise again. Nearly all the enemy forces were miraculously obliterated. Timid Gideon proved to be a heroic leader after all. That, however, is only part of the story.

Alas, a handful of episodes remain in Gideon's tale, nearly all less endearing than the last. Not satisfied with delivering Israel from her enemies, Gideon prosecuted a crusade of personal revenge. Along the way, he made enemies of his brothers east of the Jordan, humiliated his own son, and reintroduced idolatry to his hometown.

- *What two towns east of the Jordan refused to help Gideon and his men (8:4–9)? What aid did he request? What did he threaten each town after their refusals?*

- *After his victory Gideon returned to these towns to carry out his vengeance against them. What evidence did he show them of his victory? How did he know whom to punish? How did his revenge against Peniel exceed his original threat (vv. 10–21)?*

- *What does this series of events say about Gideon the underdog?*

The tribes west of the Jordan cooperated with the offensive against the eastern raiders, but Sukkoth and Peniel on the east bank did not. The elders of Sukkoth indicated that they were not confident that Gideon would succeed in capturing the Midianite kings. They seemed afraid that if they helped Gideon's men press the attack and these kings were *not* subdued, the kings' vengeance would fall on them. In this regard, Peniel was even more exposed than Sukkoth.

The response of these two towns reveals that Israel was not a federal nation-state. Instead, they were as loyal to one another as they chose to be. Gideon did not command contributions as the nation's official leader. He requested help for his men, who were tired but still pursuing the remaining Midianite enemies. He was turned down flat.

On his successful return, Gideon punished the elders of Sukkoth with thorns. He probably had the elders stripped and bound then lashed with whips braided with jagged thorns harvested from the local landscape. Then, besides destroying the watchtower at Peniel, he also brutally massacred all the men of the town. That bloodbath revealed the heart of a leader drunk on his own power.

- *Who witnessed Gideon's vengeance on his own people? How were they captured (vv. 10–12)?*

- *What were the numbers of fighters in that battle? How did Gideon win?*

• *After watching Gideon's barbarity, what expectations do you think the kings had for their own lives? What previous crime did they confess to (vv. 18–19)? What was Gideon's motive for chasing these men all the way across the Jordan and into their own territory?*

• *Whom did Gideon command to execute these kings (vv. 20–21)? Why did he not follow through? Can you see any of the underdog Gideon's nature in this young man?*

- *How do the two kings taunt Gideon as they are staring down the point of his sword? What does this tell us about these warriors?*

This episode shows us that personal revenge motivated Gideon's campaign across the Jordan. We learn that these men and their fighters had cut down Gideon's own brothers in a previous battle (maybe in one of the raids of 6:1–6). In retaliation, Gideon cut down the Midianites and claimed their possessions.

Revenge is a dangerous business. It orients a person's thoughts and efforts on past offenses, keeping him from thriving in the present. Furthermore, it creates a back-and-forth, tit-for-tat feud without a natural end. Often this cycle of offense expands to include others into concentric circles of pain. The godly alternative to vengeance is kindness and forgiveness. God's people have always been called to this (Exodus 23:4; 2 Chronicles 28:14–15; Proverbs 25:21–22), but Christians should specialize in it.

Christians know the surprising mercy of God. When our Lord was hanging on the cross, he prayed for the forgiveness of his enemies (Luke 23:34). When we were his enemies, God took all the necessary steps to reconcile with us through Jesus (Romans 5:10). He taught us to love our enemies (Luke 6:27–29).

If we drop our demand for vengeance, does that mean people will never face justice for the wrongs they have done to us? Not at all. In fact, it puts justice in the hands of the only one who is perfectly just (2 Thessalonians 1:6–7). Like Paul wrote to the Romans, "Never hold a grudge or try to get even...Beloved, don't be obsessed with taking revenge, but leave that to God's righteous justice. For the Scriptures say: 'Vengeance is mine, and I will repay,' says the Lord" (Romans 12:17, 19). Forgiving our enemies shows that we trust God to deal righteously with those who mistreat us.

Declining a Dynasty

• *After the liberation, what honor did Israel offer to Gideon in gratitude (Judges 8:22–23)? How did he react to this honor? What spiritual principle did he emphasize in his response?*

• *What request did he make instead (vv. 24–27)? What did he make from the gold? What ironic tragedy resulted from producing this artifact?*

• *Compare what Gideon did and made to Exodus 32:1–6. What similarities do you see?*

The Israelites would have made him king and given his family a dynasty if he wanted it. The Lord predicted the Israelites would want a human king after they inherited their own land (Deuteronomy 17:14–15). The desire may have crossed their minds before, but this was the first time they expressed it openly.

The offer would have been tempting to many leaders, but Gideon did not jump at the opportunity to rule. Israel didn't need another ruler, he reasoned, because it already had one. The Lord was and should always be their king. Still, the allure of a human king was real, and the desire for one would grow throughout the period of the judges and into the life of Samuel (1 Samuel 8:4–9).

Instead of assuming the royal throne, Gideon asked for some of the plunder from the battles. His request was small, only an earring from each man, so they gladly gave it. Altogether, those earrings weighed a little more than forty pounds. It was enough for a fine shirt, or ephod, of gold chain mail, a fitting tribute to the courage of the reluctant underdog and the miraculous victory of God.

Ephods were at least implicitly religious. In Scripture, priests typically wore this type of garment as they performed their religious duties of representing the people to God and God to the people. Priests would wear the ephod when they sought God's will, when they made sacrifices, and when they led worship at the tabernacle. By making this garment, Gideon imitated a priestly role.

No sooner had he placed this memorial garment on display in his hometown than the Israelites began to treat it as an idol. They probably believed that they could seek the Lord through this ephod. So they came to Ophrah to worship and idolized a shirt made of enemy earrings. Apparently, Gideon permitted this blasphemy, and he and his family may have participated in it. He was the one who dismantled the idol shrines there. Now he had installed a new one.

- *How long was the peace of Gideon (Judges 8:28)? How many sons did Gideon and his many wives produce (vv. 29–32)?*

- *One of his offspring is singled out for mention. Who? How was he related to Gideon?*

- *What practices did the Israelites return to after Gideon died (vv. 33–35)? What two individuals did they break faith with?*

DIGGING DEEPER

Because of his great grace, the Lord brought Israel out from under the oppressive rule of Pharaoh, the king of Egypt. Dramatically, miraculously, God began to personally rule over them in power and love. That is why they proclaimed about him on the day he saved them through the Red Sea, "The LORD reigns for ever and ever" (Exodus 15:18 NIV). Pharaoh was temporary; their King was eternal.

Even when a human king reigned, Israel continued to worship YAHWEH as their ultimate King. Earthly kings might rule their nations from thrones in Jerusalem, Damascus, Nineveh, Babylon, or Egypt, but the Lord reigns everywhere from heaven (Isaiah 6:1–6; 66:1–2). Devout believers in all kingdoms and all times know this is true. We acknowledge it in our prayers and in our praise.

For example, Sir Robert Grant was born in India in 1799, the son of the director of the East India Company. A lawyer, member of parliament, governor of Bombay, and supporter of evangelical world missions, he lived a vibrant activist Christian life in service to the king of Britain and the King of the universe. In 1833, Grant wrote these lyrics, which weren't published until after his death:

> O worship the King, All glorious above,
> And gratefully sing His power and His love;
> Our Shield and Defender, the Ancient of Days,
> Pavilioned in splendor, and girded with praise.

- *Look up the following verses and match them to the beginning phrases in the middle column and the ending phrases in right-hand column. Take special note of how acknowledging the Lord as King leads to worship and submission to his will.*

This Scripture...	...begins with...	...and ends...
Psalm 10:16	____ The Lord God Most High is astonishing, awesome beyond words!	____ he is the living God, the eternal King.
Psalm 24:8	____ The LORD will be king over the whole earth.	____ he will save us completely.
Psalm 47:2	____ The kingdom of the world has become the kingdom of our God and of his Anointed One!	____ his kingdom rules the entire universe.
Psalm 103:19	____ You, YAHWEH, are King forever and ever!	____ Turn your lives back to God and put your trust in the hope-filled gospel!
Psalm 145:13	____ You ask, "Who is this King of Glory?"	____ He will reign supreme for an eternity of eternities!
Isaiah 33:22	____ It is time for God's kingdom to be experienced in its fullness!	____ On that day there will be one LORD, and his name the only name.
Jeremiah 10:10*	____ YAHWEH has established his throne in heaven;	____ through all the ages of time and eternity!
Zechariah 14:9*	____ The Lord YAHWEH is our Judge, our Lawgiver, and our King	____ YAHWEH, armed and ready for battle, YAHWEH, invincible in every way!
Mark 1:15	____ But the LORD is the true God;	____ He's the formidable and powerful King over all the earth.
Revelation 11:15	____ You are the Lord who reigns over your never-ending kingdom	____ All the nations will perish from your land.

*New International Version

 EXPERIENCE GOD'S HEART

- *God's sovereign intervention so overwhelmed Gideon that he worshiped. When have you been compelled personally to worship? What were the circumstances? Was it a new understanding, a supernatural experience, divine protection or provision, or something else?*

- *Is it easier for you to forgive or to hold a grudge? How often do you notice that you harbor resentment or hostility toward others who have wronged you? What would it take for you to pray, "Father, forgive them"?*

♥ SHARE GOD'S HEART

- *The Lord limited Gideon's forces so that no one would think the battle was won without the Lord's help. If you have been in Christ for a while, you probably have had an experience where your meager resources were not enough for the task, but God did it anyway. Share a personal story like that with a younger Christian.*

- *Jesus told his disciples to interrupt their public worship if they realized they might have wronged someone (Matthew 5:23–24). Part of the cure for revenge is being able to forgive or seek forgiveness. Have you wronged someone who needs to hear a sincere apology? Do it before the next time you go to church.*

Talking It Out

1. In your group, try to name as many worship songs as you can about the Lord being our King. Choose one to sing together.

2. Big churches, big businesses, big cities, big armies. Discuss what it is about bigness that is so desirable and why we tend to disparage small things.

3. Discuss times when small things made a significant difference.

4. The story of Gideon shows us some ways that God confirmed his will. Recall from Scripture other ways God confirmed what he wanted his followers to do. Has he used any of these ways to guide you? If so, share the story.

LESSON 6

Israel's First King

(Judges 9)

People become famous for many reasons, but they are *infamous* for villainy. Think for a moment and a dozen fictional or historical villains easily come to mind. We remember villains. We remember the names of mass shooters but seldom the names of their victims. We remember war crimes defendants but not their prosecutors. We remember notorious outlaws but usually forget the lawmen who bring them down or bring them in.

Biblically, we remember Pilate, Herod, and Caiaphas, but the names of other regional governors are not even recorded. Every Christian knows the name of Judas, but many cannot name the disciples Lebbeus or Nathanael. Unless characters distinguish themselves by virtue or evil, they go unnoticed. Thus, it was with Gideon's family and his *infamous* son Abimelech.

- *How many brothers did Abimelech have (Judges 8:29–32)? How was his upbringing different from that of his brothers?*

Gideon's noble rejection of kingship was tainted by the life he lived thereafter. He wanted the benefits of royalty without the title. He took many wives, for example, and sired many children—seventy sons, not to mention his daughters. Besides his official wives, he also took a concubine from the nearby town of Shechem.

In the ancient Middle East, concubines were commonplace. Abraham and his brother Nahor each had a concubine. Jacob had two concubines. A concubine was a female slave or mistress with whom a man was lawfully permitted to have sexual intercourse. Sometimes this relationship came about due to a wife's infertility, as in the case of Abraham and Sarah. Any children the concubine bore would be reckoned as legitimate. By the time of Israel's first kings, the practice seems to have been limited to royalty. For example, kings Saul, David, and Solomon had concubines. Solomon had three hundred of them!

When Gideon rejected the opportunity to rule over Israel as king, it didn't keep him from living like a king. His concubine gave birth to yet another son, and Gideon gave him the name Abimelech. His name means "My Father Is King" or "Heir to the Throne." Abimelech was an ancient title dating back to the kings of the Philistines in the days of Abraham and Isaac (Genesis 20:2; 26:1). The leader of each generation was called the *Abimelech*.

- *What argument did Abimelech make to the people of Shechem that he should be their king (Judges 9:1–4)? Why did the people agree with him?*

• *What did they give him as evidence of their support? What did he do with this gift?*

Unlike his father Gideon, Abimelech was eager for the title. If you name a child "Heir to the Throne," who would be shocked when he expects to be the king? Shortly after the death of Gideon, Abimelech connived to seize the leadership of Israel, beginning with Shechem. With the cooperation of his mother's relations and neighbors, he secured the resources he needed to stage a take-over. It would take a dangerous group of thugs to pull it off.

• *What was Abimelech's first act as leader of this Shechem-supported band of ruffians (9:5–6)? Was he 100 percent successful in his evil mission? Why would he take such a violent, drastic step?*

• *Once Abimelech dispatched his rivals, what did the city of Shechem do for him?*

Was Gideon right or wrong to refuse the monarchy? It is a question worth pondering, especially with the benefit of hindsight. The world will never know how things might have been different if Gideon had agreed to be king. Probably, Gideon's oldest son, Jether, would have led Israel after him. That timid son who refused violence (8:20–21) certainly would have done things differently than Abimelech. Instead, on this dreadful day, his skull was smashed on a single stone along with almost all of Gideon's sons.

- *Explain Jotham's parable (9:7–21). What do you think it means? What does the sequence of refusals to rule indicate about Gideon and his sons? How is Gideon's legacy referred to in his rebuke? Was this a divine curse or the bitter wish of an angry, grieving brother?*

- *Who disturbed the confidence that the people of Shechem had in Abimelech (vv. 22–25)? Why did he do it? How was this shift in sentiment a kind of poetic justice for both the king and his city?*

• *What did the people of Shechem do to undermine public safety under Abimelech's rule?*

Abimelech betrayed his father and his father's family when he murdered his brothers. The city of Shechem partnered with him in this treachery. Without that support, he never would have embarked on his bloody campaign. The betrayal that bubbled up from that city was a fitting consequence for Abimelech. Soon, this fraying alliance would destroy them too.

 # DIGGING DEEPER

So much damage was done when Adam and Eve were taken in by the deceit of the Evil One (Genesis 3).[10] From the first generation of human beings, treachery has been part of our sinful story—when someone who should be loyal trades sides, when someone who should be faithful proves false. Who doesn't have a friend or family member who has deceived them?

Betrayal cuts deeply because it is personal. As the songwriter Michael Card has penned, "Only a friend can betray a friend; a stranger has nothing to gain."[11] The injured party has a reasonable expectation that he will suffer no wrong from a friend, so he is usually surprised when the injury comes.

Jesus told his disciples that they could expect betrayals. Following him will realign our loyalties and the loyalties of those who once loved us. Though he wasn't surprised by betrayal, he also experienced it, so he understands our suffering when it happens to us.

- *The following passages are a small sampling of biblical betrayals. Jot down details of the betrayed, the betrayer, and the betrayal.*

	Betrayed	Betrayer	Betrayal
Genesis 4:3–10			
Genesis 27:30–41			
Genesis 34:11–29			
Judges 4:17–21			
2 Samuel 3:26–39			
2 Samuel 11:1–17			
2 Samuel 15:1–10			
2 Samuel 18:5–15			
Daniel 6:1–16			
Matthew 10:21–28			
Luke 22:1–6, 47–48			

- *Describe the newcomer who brought these hostilities to a head (Judges 9:26–29). What were his obvious character flaws? What boast did he make about his own leadership potential? What ancient leader of the city was mentioned?*

- *Who reported these threats to Abimelech (vv. 30–41)? What was his role in the city (v. 28)? What military strategy did he suggest for countering this insurgency?*

- *How did Zebul keep Gaal from acting soon enough against Abimelech's forces? How did he taunt Gaal on the verge of his defeat?*

- *Where did the battle take place? Who ultimately routed Abimelech's enemies from Shechem?*

Treachery in Shechem

Shechem is an ancient city first mentioned when Abraham relocated from Ur (Genesis 12:6–7). At Shechem he built his first altar to worship the Lord in Canaan. From that point on, this city was important to Israel. Jacob returned there after his lengthy exile (Genesis 33:18–20). It became the location of the tabernacle (Joshua 8:30–35; 24:1–2), the burial place for Israel's patriarchs (Joshua 24:32; Acts 7:15–16), the inauguration site of kings (1 Kings 12:1), and the first capital of the Northern Kingdom of Israel (v. 25).

When Israel's forefather Jacob lived nomadically near Shechem, his daughter Dinah was kidnapped and raped by the son of the city's leader Hamor (Genesis 34). This entitled rapist, Shechem, was named after the city. After his abuse of Dinah, Shechem insisted that she become his wife. The mistreatment of their sister incensed Jacob's sons, and they connived to retaliate. They convinced Hamor and Shechem that the match could only be made if the men of the city would all become circumcised. Then, while the men were still recovering from this painful ritual, the brothers swooped into town, slaughtered them all, and recovered Dinah.

Gaal referred to this episode in his great drunken boasts (Judges 9:28). He recalled Shechem's Canaanite forebearers, Shechem and Hamor, and demanded to know why the people of the city were willing to be ruled by the half-Jew Abimelech. Even after the sentiment of the city turned against Abimelech, there remained a loyal deputy. Gaal mocked him in his drunken boasts as well. But Zebul could not tolerate this outrage against the king, so he schemed for Gaal's defeat. Shechem had an old relationship with treachery.

- *How did Abimelech and his band take revenge against the city of Shechem (9:42–49)? How complete was their defeat? How did Abimelech deal with the people holed up in their fortress? How did they try to make Shechem unlivable and unusable in the future?*

 # DIGGING DEEPER

The mention of idolatry in Judges 8 and 9 is when the people flee to the tower of their false god Baal-Berith (8:33; 9:27, 46). They ran there because it was an obvious defensive structure. No swords, arrows, or spears could penetrate its walls. Besides that, maybe there would be a little spiritual protection from the god they were devoted to. But the people ran to their false god for refuge only to be consumed by fire. Poignant. Tragic.

On the other hand, the Lord is called Israel's fortress, refuge, and strong tower almost one hundred times in the Old Testament. He protected them against enemies, provided shelter in trouble, and proved a reliable stability in uncertain times. Furthermore, the Bible assures his faithful people that their faithful God will never disappoint them.

- *Look up the following passages: Deuteronomy 32:36–38; 2 Samuel 22:2–3; Psalms 27:1–5; 46:1–7; 62:1–8; Proverbs 18:10; Isaiah 28:13–15; 30:1–5; 44:16–20; Joel 3:16–17. Place those describing God, our true refuge, on the left and summarize the message of each. Place those describing the false hope of false gods on the right and summarize them.*

The Lord Our Refuge		False Hope of False Gods	

- *What further campaign of violence did Abimelech carry out (Judges 9:50–55)? What tactic did he try to repeat at the tower of refuge in Thebez?*

- *Who saved the citizens of that city from him? How? How is this a kind of poetic justice for Abimelech? How did he try to avoid the humiliation of Sisera (5:24–27)?*

- *Why did Abimelech's rule unravel the way that it did (9:56–57)? How were all these deadly encounters the fulfillment of Jotham's curse (v. 20)?*

Ironically, a single stone finished this ruthless hothead and his reign over Israel. Like his brothers, Abimelech's skull was crushed by a stone. A woman lethally wounded this warrior, like the enemy Sisera. Not even the quick sword of his servant could erase this embarrassing fact. The Lord punished him and the people of Shechem for the turmoil and violence they had perpetrated.

King Cravings

Honorable or not, Abimelech was Israel's first human king. Proverbs 20:28 tells us, "Good leadership is built on love and truth, for kindness and integrity are what keep leaders in their position of trust." Without those virtues, Abimelech's reign was always precarious. He relished the power and prominence kingship provided, but he did not possess the character necessary for the role.

Abimelech did not wisely settle disputes. He did not seek the well-being of his people. He did not lead them together toward common goals. He didn't even defend them well against oppressors. He ended up destroying the one city that offered him its allegiance. By the time of his death, Israel needed Judge Tola to arise and rescue them from this chaos (Judges 10:1–2). Maybe having a king was a bad idea after all.

After Abimelech, it would be hundreds of years before the people lobbied for another king. Maybe he cured them of their king craving. Maybe they would be better off having no ruler at all than to endure a bloodbath like they got from Abimelech.

Then again, Israel's experience also revealed that they were vulnerable and anchorless without a leader. Judges could course-correct for a while, but they were, by nature, temporary leaders. As soon as one judge left the scene, Israel plunged into idolatry again until the next oppression (2:19). There is something of this in the offer of a dynasty to Gideon. They needed a godly leader who would abide with them. The cycle of sin had them in its grasp, and only a permanent deliverer could rescue them.

What if the deliverer weren't so flawed? What if his reign

could last forever? By starts and stumbles, the seeds of longing for a righteous eternal King were planted in the hearts of the Israelites.

 EXPERIENCE GOD'S HEART

- *Abimelech had more ambition than character. Philippians 2:3 teaches us to avoid selfish ambition to pursue the character of Christ. But we know that some ambition is good. For example, applying for a promotion is usually a good thing. However, stepping on people to get the promotion, that's a bad thing. How would you distinguish between healthy ambition and selfish ambition?*

- *Think of a time when someone betrayed you. What were the circumstances? How close was the relationship before that event? How long did it take to recover emotionally from that blow? Did you ever reconcile with that person? Is it possible to do so now? If it is still painful, ask the Lord to heal you. If you feel jaded because of it, ask the Lord to soften your heart again.*

♥ SHARE GOD'S HEART

• *Tell someone about a time you experienced the Lord as a refuge. It may be an instance of physical, spiritual, or relationship protection. Whatever attacks come our way, YAHWEH is well able to rescue us.*

• *Write a letter or email to a local leader (such as a school board member, city councilperson, town administrator, or police officer) to encourage them. They almost always hear from disgruntled or hostile constituents. Think of a specific quality or position you appreciate and thank them for it. Tell them you are praying for their leadership.*

Talking It Out

1. Abimelech saw an opportunity to clamber to the top of the pile, over the corpses of better men than himself. The combination of power and corruption destroyed him. Our world is full of influential leaders who lack virtue. Discuss this with your group. Why does it seem that the people who aspire to power are often the ones least qualified to wield it?

2. Our rulers often fail us. They make empty promises to get our hopes and our votes. They achieve a position of power only to prove they can't handle it. We often vent to one another about these disappointments. What if we took a different tack? What if we talked to one another about how these shortcomings make us eager for the Lord's return? What if the dashing of our hopes in humans made us even more hopeful in the Lord? What if the moral or wisdom failures of people prompted us to praise God for his perfections? Talk about how we could take this tack together.

LESSON 7

The Young and the Reckless
(Judges 10–12)

Mercifully, the era of Abimelech ended after only a few years, and the stable place-holder leadership of Tola (Judges 10:1–2) and Jair (vv. 3–5) gave Israel forty-five years for recovery and renewal. Rather than take advantage of that, the Israelites renewed only their unfaithfulness to YAHWEH.

- *Review again the Cycle of Sin and Deliverance in Lesson 1. After reading Judges 10:6–10, where would you place the Israelites at this point in their history? What specific apostasy were they committing?*

- *What two violent words describe their treatment under the Philistine and Ammonite tormentors (v. 8)? How long did their domination last before Israel acknowledged their sin?*

- *Describe the unusual answer from the Lord when Israel pleaded for his help. What further earnestness did the Israelites show in seeking God? What finally moved him to act (vv. 11–16)?*

Again, the Lord's answer to their rebellion was discipline brought by their surrounding neighbors. The tribes on the east side of the Jordan River were threatened by the Ammonites. In their aggression, they even crossed the Jordan and harried the tribes in central Israel. In the southwest, the Philistines began to trouble Israel.

YAHWEH was unmoved by their prayers. He had heard all these words before. Like the spouse of a serial adulterer, he did not trust their promises or their assurances that things would be different this time. In fact, he sent them back to their favorite idols, urging Israel to call out to them for salvation.

⚡ DIGGING DEEPER

The Bible describes idolatry as adultery, even prostitution. It's a personal, intimate sin against the Lord. To God, pagan idolatry was not merely faulty religious ceremonies, theological heresy, or an alternative worldview. None of these carry the raw emotion of spiritual infidelity. To the Lord, idolatry is heartfelt rejection and betrayal of him. It was the deep pain of marital unfaithfulness felt by a jilted husband.

God commanded his prophet Hosea to live out this metaphor. God told him to marry and start a family with a prostitute (Hosea 1:2–3), knowing she would be unfaithful to Hosea. She went back to her life of sexual immorality even while they were married (2:1–23). Then God told him to go to her again, to find her on the auction block (3:1), and to buy her back for himself (vv. 2–3). Hosea took this prostitute home again as his wife in a graphic display of YAHWEH's faithfulness to an unfaithful people.

- *While Hosea is the most explicit example of this principle, both Old and New Testaments warn us not to follow the unfaithful example of Israel. Read the following passages and take note of the situation and the emotional impact on the Lord and his beloved.*

	Emotional Words and Phrases
Exodus 34:14	
Leviticus 26:40–42	
Deuteronomy 31:16–18	
Psalm 106:36–46	
Isaiah 1:21–26	
Jeremiah 3:6–11	
Ezekiel 16:30–34	
Matthew 12:38–42	
Mark 8:34–38	
James 4:4–6	

Mission of Mercy

John the Baptist challenged the religious phonies of his day to "prove your repentance by a changed life" (Matthew 3:8). Sincerity would show in the way they lived.

Eventually, the Israelites surpassed mere words with outward steps to show their repentance. They took down their pagan altars and worshiped the Lord again. Still, the text indicates that while these pious actions were a step in the right direction, it was ultimately God's compassion for his people in misery that motivated him to save them.

God is motivated by mercy. He knows what we deserve: the just punishment for sin. But when we finally acknowledge what we deserve, he withholds it and saves us instead. "When the extraordinary compassion of God our Savior and his overpowering love suddenly appeared in person...he came to save us. Not because of any virtuous deed that we have done but only because of his extravagant mercy" (Titus 3:4–5). "God, please, in your mercy and because of the blood sacrifice, forgive me, for I am nothing but the most miserable of all sinners" (Luke 18:13) is always the right prayer for those in need of a rescue.

This time, God's rescue began east of the Jordan River in the mountainous northern region of Gilead. This was the region where Judge Jair had ruled for more than two decades. In his absence, the Ammonites aggressively tormented the people of the tribes of Gad and Manasseh. These inhabitants were eager to recruit a hero, and God was ready to move.

- *What reward were the people of Gilead willing to give to the champion who would lead them against Ammon (Judges 10:17–18)? Whom did they approach to lead this campaign (11:4–11)?*

- *What detail in Jephthah's backstory set him apart from his brothers (11:1–3)? How did his brothers treat him as a result? Absent a supportive family, what kind of people did Jephthah take up with?*

- *For what reasons might Jephthah have doubted the proposal of the leaders from Gilead? What assurances did he demand? What assurances did they give?*

Another damaged family produced another broken judge. Like Abimelech before him, Jephthah was the illegitimate son of a prominent family. His presence in the family caused inheritance problems, so his siblings exiled him. Now, however, they needed this mighty warrior, so it was time to eat their words.

Once Jephthah had confidence that the people were behind him, he confronted Ammon's king. In a superb example of rivalling histories, each side laid out its case for their territorial claims. Jephthah may have been a mighty warrior surrounded by brigands, but he was also a capable, if not persuasive, historian.

- *How did Jephthah initiate the confrontation with the king of Ammon (11:12–22)? How did the Ammonite explain the roots of the conflict? How did Jephthah's view differ? On what basis did he disagree?*

- *Review the account of Israel's first conflicts in this territory (Numbers 21:21–35). In the Bible's telling, who were the aggressors? What steps did Israel take to avoid the conflict? How was it resolved?*

- *What challenges did Jephthah put to the king's claims (Judges 11:23–28)? What comparisons does he make between the Lord and Ammon's false god Chemosh?*

- *What other regional king from history did Jephthah mention? How does his story make Jephthah's point?*

- *How did Ammon's king respond to this history lesson?*

Battle of the Gods

To Jephthah, this dispute was not merely a contest between two peoples. It was also a battle between their deities. It was nothing short of miraculous when the infant nation of Israel, with no military or battle experience, conquered the established nations determined to wipe them out. They were not even there to take or claim land but merely to pass through on their way to Canaan. Jephthah and the Israelites rightly saw this territory as a divine gift from the Lord.

Besides, Ammon and Moab had their own god, Chemosh, a vile god whom the people worshiped with ritual sex and child sacrifice. Jephthah wondered why Ammon did not simply accept the land that their own god parceled out to them. Surely, they could be content with that.

Frequently, Scripture also refers to Chemosh as the Baal of

Peor (Lord of Peor, the highest mountain in Moab). As such, the Moabites worshiped him under King Balak (Numbers 22–24). Balak hired the magician Balaam to pronounce a curse on embryonic Israel, but after seeing what they did to Sihon and Og, he did not dare go to war directly with them. The Lord would not allow Balaam to pronounce the curse, so the land remained in Israel's possession.

Throughout his argument, Jephthah grounded his territorial claims in the power of Israel's God. The Lord empowered Israel to take the land in the first place. He also enabled them to keep the land over the centuries. And the Lord would empower Jephthah to drive these Ammonite invaders out of the land they demanded.

- *What unique empowerment did Jephthah have when he advanced against the Ammonites (Judges 11:29–33)? How did the battle conclude?*

- *What gesture of sincerity did Jephthah make in seeking the Lord's favor in battle? Was this measure necessary to win the victory? Did the Lord demand it?*

• *How was this great victory spoiled by grief (vv. 34–40)? Evaluate the character quality of Jephthah and his daughter in this interaction. Which one appears to be measured and mature? Which was reckless and self-absorbed?*

• *What accommodation did Jephthah's daughter request? What was she grieving over? How did her sacrifice inspire an annual remembrance?*

With the supernatural enabling of God's Spirit, Jephthah attacked the Ammonite invaders. Thus empowered, he had all the resources he needed to win a great victory, but on the cusp of that victory, this mighty warrior made a mighty mistake. In keeping with Israel's recent idolatry and taking a cue from Israel's pagan neighbors, he promised a sacrifice to entice the Lord to fight on his behalf. It was reckless, unnecessary bargaining with God.

The foregone victory was followed by forlorn grief when Jephthah's only daughter danced out to meet him in celebration. According to his foolish, gratuitous vow, she would become the sacrifice. While he came undone, she agreed to the terms but requested time to grieve for her unfulfilled future.

Scholars have debated whether Jephthah actually sacrificed his daughter. Theologically, it is an appalling possibility. The Lord prohibited Israel from sacrificing their children (Leviticus 20:2–5; Deuteronomy 18:10), so how could he allow it here? To solve this dilemma, some suggest that Jephthah's daughter merely pledged perpetual virginity, rather like a cloistered nun. Doing so, they argue, she sacrificed the generations that might come after her and, in effect, ended Jephthah's family.[12] While this solution would make the narrative more palatable for the Christian reader, there is no indication of it in the text. As sickening as it may be, it is most likely that Jephthah performed a human sacrifice.

Like Jephthah, even devout believers are profoundly influenced by the society we live in. Witness the trends in what is acceptable moral and cultural behavior among Christians in Western societies today. The compromises we tolerate would appall our ancestors and our descendants. We have not reasoned our way to this compromise. We have absorbed it like environmental pollutants, unaware of the transformation happening in our souls. It is the cultural atmosphere we breathe.

Like the people he had just defeated, like his own people who worshiped the gods of the Ammonites, Jephthah sacrificed his daughter. This pagan ceremony seemed tragic but reasonable to a leader of such a spiritually adulterous nation. She was not the only Israelite Jephthah would kill.

War of the Words

"What do you call this?" shouted the soldier as he held up a sprig of parsley to each villager he interrogated. If the stranger failed to pronounce the word *perejil* with the Spanish trilled-*r* sound to the questioner's satisfaction, he was taken aside and killed. In less than a week, more than twenty thousand Haitians were identified and massacred this way. The Dominican Parsley Massacre of 1937 is a twentieth-century example of the military use of *shibboleths*. The first known example was under the anti-Ephraim campaign of Jephthah.

- *What complaint did the Ephraimites have against Jephthah (Judges 12:1–7)? What threat did they make? How did Jephthah respond to that threat? What further insult did the Ephraimites hurl at the people of Gilead?*

- *What well-worn strategy did the warriors of Gilead use against Ephraim? How did they identify the Ephraimites for slaughter?*

As with Gideon, the Ephraimites were offended by their exclusion from this victory across the Jordan (8:1). In answer to their threat to burn his house down around him, Jephthah strapped on his sword and went to war. Besides threatening Jephthah, the warriors of Ephraim insulted all the Gileadites as *renegades*. This Hebrew word can also be rendered *turncoats* or *fugitives*, soldiers fleeing from a battle. So the men of Gilead were only too eager to prove their courage in battle.

Jephthah's men seized the fords of the Jordan and killed any Ephraimites trying to cross over. Their similar clothing and appearance could not camouflage them. Their accents were the giveaway. An American cannot hide in Ireland. An Australian cannot blend in among Canadians unnoticed. A Texan stands out in

Boston. Even though they share a language, their identity is obvious when they open their mouths. The initial letter in *shibboleth* identified the Ephraimites, and tens of thousands of them died in this Israelite civil war.

Ephraim was devastated by their own words and not just the way they pronounced them. By taking offense in the first place, by threatening and insulting their brothers, they stoked hostility that resulted in their own bloody defeat. If they had held their tongues, things might have turned out differently.

Furthermore, the Gileadites were too ready to take offense. When one cannot bear an insult with grace, a conflict can brew out of control. When confrontation finally happens, the consequences can be terrible. Then, when the hostility dies down, it only simmers until the next opportunity to fight. There is no obvious end to the reprisals.

As St. Paul wrote, Jesus taught us a different way:

> You find God's favor by deciding to please
> God even when you endure hardships
> because of unjust suffering. For what merit
> is it to endure mistreatment for wrongdoing?
> Yet if you are mistreated when you do what
> is right, and you faithfully endure it, this
> is commendable before God. In fact, you
> were called to live this way, because Christ
> also suffered in your place, leaving you his
> example for you to follow.
>
> > He never sinned
> > and he never spoke deceitfully.
>
> > When he was verbally abused, he did not
> > return with an insult; when he suffered, he
> > would not threaten retaliation. Jesus faithfully
> > entrusted himself into the hands of God, who
> > judges righteously. (1 Peter 2:19–23)

This episode in Judges 12 shows us the dangerous divisions

that existed within the nation of Israel. Tribalism and violence against one another were as dangerous to them as the oppression of neighboring peoples. Even when the yoke of external bondage was broken, they still had to deal with internal conflicts. In spiritual unfaithfulness and generational unforgiveness, the Israelites were their own worst enemies.

The Shibboleth of Salvation

Even though the shibboleth strategy led to carnage, we should note that the shibboleth also saved. Only the hostile Ephraimites were singled out by the way they uttered this word. For the Gileadites and most Israelites, speaking the shibboleth kept them from judgment.

Christians will see a parallel here in our genuine heartfelt confession of faith. As the apostle Paul tells us, "If you publicly declare with your mouth that Jesus is Lord and believe in your heart that God raised him from the dead, you will experience salvation. The heart that believes in him receives the gift of the righteousness of God—and then the mouth confesses, resulting in salvation...And it's true: 'Everyone who calls on the Lord's name will experience new life'" (Romans 10:9–10, 13). Confessing Jesus as Lord saves.

However, the rescue is not merely the words we say but how we say them. A false confession is obvious to the Lord. In Matthew 7:21–23, Jesus explained that our "pronunciation" of this truth must come from a genuine transformed heart: "Not everyone who says to me, 'Lord, Lord,' will enter into heaven's kingdom. It is only those who persist in doing the will of my heavenly Father" (v. 21).

- *What town was Judge Ibzan from (Judges 12:8–10)? What unique arrangements did he make for his children's marriages? Why do you think he did that?*

- *How long did Elon judge Israel (vv. 11–12)? What did Judge Abdon have in common with Gideon (vv. 13–15)?*

🖤 EXPERIENCE GOD'S HEART

Many a frightened and insincere prayer is uttered in a moment of danger. In a battle zone, a financial disaster, a family crisis, or legal trouble, we tend to bargain with God. We make unwise promises in the moment, hoping to sway him. Sometimes we follow through. Sometimes we forget about it once the desperation passes.

- *Can you remember an instance like this in your own life? Did God answer your prayers? Did you keep your desperate promises? Do you regret making them? Confess these things and thank God for his mercy. That's what really motivates him.*

Jephthah's young daughter paid a high price for his reckless vow, but she submitted to this injustice admirably. Knowing that the decision was out of her hands, she entrusted herself to the Lord. Jesus did the same when he faced injustice.

- *What injustice do you face that is out of your hands? Is it political, cultural, legal, or relational? Are you inclined to resist or accept the situation? What would it look like for you to trust the Lord and follow in Jesus' steps?*

 SHARE GOD'S HEART

- *Broken families produce broken people. Trauma, abuse, neglect, and rejection lead to damaged self-images and the inability to trust. Awareness of this can help us understand broken people in our lives. Maybe you know someone broken by their family of origin. Pause and pray for them.*

We can only break the cycle of retribution by forgiveness. No amount of tit-for-tat will ever satisfy. However, if someone refuses to return the insult or throw another punch, there is hope of resolution. If someone absorbs the injury and offers forgiveness instead, healing can happen.

- *Identify someone who has hurt you. Ask for God's help to forgive them. If it is appropriate, pray for a way to communicate forgiveness to them.*

Talking It Out

1. Since cultural conformity usually happens without our awareness, it can be helpful to discuss this concept with others. In your group, brainstorm about shifting moral and cultural values. What sinful conformity might be happening that we don't notice without help? What areas are most prone to compromise? Allow the freedom to disagree with one another about the issues.

2. It is easy enough to recognize hostility toward believers from the world around us. It is a little trickier to pinpoint ways that we are dangerous to one another. Discuss some of the ways we create conflict with one another inside the Christian movement and what we can do about it.

LESSON 8

The Original Avenger

(Judges 13–16)

Tales from the Marvel Cinematic Universe have become the most successful film franchise ever, tripling the revenue from the highest-grossing rival. Beginning with *Iron Man* in 2008, the MCU has churned out more than thirty movies, about two per year. Millions of viewers have been transfixed by more than the supernatural exploits of comic book superheroes. By presenting characters with their tragic origin stories, their personal flaws, and the heroes' intramural conflicts, the personal lives of the Avengers draw fans in.

In this action series, Captain America is called the First Avenger. Perhaps that is true in the MCU. But the Bible presents an incredible hulk of a warrior whose life revolved around vengeance, from his origin story straight through to his endgame. His epic feats and his tragic flaws still captivate us today. This Hebrew hulk was the original avenger, Samson.

- *Why did God allow the Philistines to remain in the land of Canaan after the original Israelite conquest (Judges 3:1–4)? Under which previous judges had the Philistines fulfilled this purpose of God (3:31; 10:6–7)?*

- *To chastise Israel for their return to evil, how long did the Lord give the Philistines power to oppress them (13:1)? Is there any indication at this point that the Israelites were repentant or calling on God to rescue them? Did God wait for Israel's humble cry for help to save them this time? What did he begin to do for them (vv. 2–5)?*

Typology in the Bible

Many figures and events in the Old Testament foreshadow the ultimate work of God in sending Jesus to save the world. Sometimes these *types* directly prefigure the person or ministry of Jesus himself such as when Abraham built an altar to sacrifice his precious son of promise (Genesis 22), creating an obvious analogy to Jesus on Calvary. Other times these types parallel other aspects of faith in him. For instance, believers' baptism is foreshadowed when Noah and his family escaped God's judgment through the water (1 Peter 3:18–22).

Samson also serves as a type. For example, many parallels exist between Samson (Judges 13) and John the Baptist (Luke 1:5–22, 57–66, 80). When the situation was dark for Yahweh's people, oppressed by foreigners in their own land and religiously adrift, God initiated his deliverance in an unexpected and miraculous way.

- *Read the origin stories of both faith heroes and notice the similarities and differences. Jot the Scripture reference that supports each statement in the space below Samson and/or John. The first one is completed for you.*

Part of the origin story of...	Samson	John
The parents were childless before the angel appeared.	*Judges 13:2*	*Luke 1:7*
The angel first appeared to the father.		
The promised child would be a son.		
The child was never to consume any grape products.		
The child was never to have his hair cut.		
The child would call his people to repentance.		
The father did not initially believe the message from God.		
The angel performed a miracle to confirm his prophetic words.		
The child was destined to deliver his people.		
The Lord named the child.		
The Spirit of the Lord was obviously active in the life of the young child.		

Samson's life began with such hope. The angelic visit, his miraculous conception, the promise of deliverance for his people, and the power of the Spirit at work in his life set this avenger apart as clearly as his Nazirite status did. However, his life became a downward spiral illustrative of Israel's own history. A distinct cycle of lust, betrayal, and vengeance led to his tragic finale.

THE BACKSTORY

Samson is the only character the Bible specifically mentions is a Nazirite, but there were others. During the ministry of the prophet Amos, many Nazirites were tempted by their own people to break their vows (Amos 2:11–12). The Hebrew root word for *Nazirite* means "separate." Any Israelite from any tribe could separate themselves to the Lord by taking a vow before the priests.

The regulations of a Nazarite vow are described in Numbers 6:1–21. In short, it meant no wine, no corpses, no razors. For most Nazirites, this level of dedication was for a pre-determined period, concluding with a sacrifice. For Samson, it was a lifelong obligation.

Two other biblical heroes were probably lifelong Nazirites. The mother of the prophet Samuel also dedicated him to the Lord before his birth, and her promise included never cutting his hair (1 Samuel 1:11, 28). John the Baptist appears to have lived as a Nazirite too. Before his birth, the angel commanded John's total abstinence from wine, and John followed this restriction throughout his ministry (Luke 1:15; Matthew 11:18–19).

Jesus, however, was not a Nazirite. He did not abstain from grapes or wine. In fact, he made wine out of water for wedding guests (John 2:6–9). He shared it with his disciples at the last supper (Mark 14:23–25). Some have mistakenly identified him as a Nazirite because of his hometown, Nazareth. Because of this, Jesus was called a Nazarene (Matthew 2:23), not a Nazirite.

Fatal Attractions

We only have a handful of episodes from Samson's decades of leadership over Israel, but each of them begins with a woman. Obviously, this powerful hero had powerful passions. His insatiable desires led to conflict, rage, and mayhem. Ultimately, they would lead to his downfall.

- *What rite of passage did Samson insist his parents initiate for him (Judges 14:1–4)? What sinful pattern was Samson repeating (3:6)?*

- *Did Samson's disobedience to Moses' law hinder God's plans? Is it comforting or troubling that God works through our rebellion to fulfill his purposes?*

- *What danger did the travelers encounter as they approached the bride's hometown (14:5–7)? How did Samson handle the crisis? How did he perform this supernatural feat of strength?*

- *What surprise did he later find at the sight of the battle (vv. 8–9)? How did this discovery become a source of conflict with his new in-laws and companions (vv. 10–15)?*

- *Who betrayed him so that they could finally win the wager against him (vv. 16–18)? How did he settle his bet (v. 19)?*

- *After Samson stormed off in a rage, what became of his wife (v. 20)? Were they reunited when his temper cooled (15:1–2)?*

- *Describe the escalating violence in the attacks and counterattacks that followed (15:3–17). What is Samson's motive in these battles? What surprising weapon did he use to do the most damage? Where is the Lord in this carnage?*

When Samson's parents indulged their son, they began a sequence of reprisals that led to a bloodbath. Being human, they could not know this, but the Lord knew. In fact, that was his intent from the start. God is sovereign over the affairs of human beings, so sovereign that even their disobedient choices serve his ultimate purposes. God wanted to strike a blow against the Philistines. He wanted to execute judgment on them. So he used the fleshly desires of his avenger to accomplish this.

What started as wedding-reception banter became a life-and-death struggle. First, thirty dead enemies were stripped of their clothes. Before long, crops were destroyed, Samson's in-laws were murdered, and a thousand warriors were massacred with a bloody jawbone. Revenge always escalates. Even this was part of the Lord's sovereign plan.

In the middle of this string of reprisals, we can see illustrations (more typology) of the Messiah Jesus. When enemies surrounded Samson (15:9–17), his own people, in cahoots with the enemy, bound and delivered him over to be killed.[13] God's champion was rejected and betrayed by his own people, but God vindicated him.

His wrath led to victory over all his enemies. No one who stood against him survived. Their hostility against the Lord's judge brought them annihilation. What Jesus did on the cross in spiritual terms, Samson did in physical battle. What the Lord will do in final judgment, Samson exemplified in history.

Perhaps it seems strange that the least Christ-like of the judges is a fertile type of Christ. On the other hand, it should be unsurprising that an Old Testament type of Christ is incomplete. After all, what human being can perfectly parallel the Savior? As a type, Samson's story points us to Jesus and creates a longing in the reader for God's ultimate triumph over his enemies.

- *What great need did Samson have after the battles (vv. 18–20)? How did Samson describe himself to God? Whom did he credit with the victory? How was his need miraculously met?*

Crashing the Gates

- *Who is the second woman mentioned in Samson's saga (16:1–3)? How did his indulgence lead him into another trap? What feat of strength did this Hebrew hulk perform to prove his invincibility against his enemies?*

Again, sexual license became a snare to Samson. While he spent the night with a Philistine prostitute, his enemies surrounded him and conspired to murder him in the morning. We do not know if he was aware of their threatening presence or simply tossing and turning with insomnia, but in the middle of the night, the superhero reminded everyone of his power.

Was Jesus thinking of this marvelous feat of strength when he promised his disciples that "the gates of hell shall not prevail against" his church (Matthew 16:18 ESV)? If so, then the crashing of the gates of Gaza provides us with another type, another picture to anticipate the unstoppable ministry of Jesus.

Victorious Defeat

- *Name the third woman Samson became entangled with (Judges 16:4–5). What was his motivation to be with her? What motivated her?*

- *What secret did Delilah want Samson to reveal (vv. 6–17)? Initially, how did he taunt her with his answers? What prediction did he repeat with each trick?*

- *What finally drove him to tell her the secret? What did he say about the Lord in this?*

- *Who would doubt what Delilah would do with this knowledge? Why do you think Samson told her anyway? What made him so susceptible to her deception?*

- *Knowing his secret, how did the Philistines capture and restrain Samson (vv. 18–21)? What surprised Samson in this ambush? What extra steps did they take to disable him?*

Some scholars believe that, by this point, Samson was weary of his role as Israel's strongman.[14] He wanted to "become as weak as anyone else" (v. 17). Throughout his life he had broken every bit of his Nazirite vows and only his hair remained of his parents' original promise. He defiled himself with countless corpses, even eating honey out of a dead carcass. Probably he drank wine at the wedding feast. He intermarried and fraternized with foreign women, clearly a snare to him.

Maybe he was tired of being different from everyone else. Maybe this was a burden even the strongman couldn't continue to carry. Maybe he just wanted to be an ordinary man in love.

We cannot know why he kept teasing Delilah with this perilous riddle, but finally the Philistines captured and enslaved Samson. With the last sign of his dedication to the Lord gone, with it went the Lord's empowering presence. In victory, the Philistines were as ruthless with him as he had been with them. They blinded and chained him to make sure he could no longer wreak justice on them. Or did they?

- *How did the Philistines celebrate their victory over the original avenger (vv. 23–24)? Whom did they credit with his defeat? How do you think Samson felt about the triumph of their god?*

- *What arrogant mistake did the Philistines make in their celebration party (vv. 25–26)?*

- *What final exploit did the blind and restrained superhero carry out (vv. 27–30)? What was he avenging? Whom did he call on for help? Which deity proved more powerful that day?*

- *Do you see any typology of Jesus Christ in the way that Samson died? What details bring to mind Jesus' suffering, death, and victory?*

- *Who recovered Samson's remains (v. 31)? What did they do with them? How long had Samson judged Israel?*

So ended the breathtaking, heartbreaking life of Israel's most conflicted judge. A vengeful avenger. A pitiless punisher. A vindictive vindicator. Never had the word *shaphat* more appropriately meant *avenger* than during the leadership of Samson.

In the biblical account, Samson never worshiped, never repented, never taught, never led others. In fact, he never even cooperated with *anyone*. He was a solitary, stubborn, selfish strongman who did nothing to change the deadly arc of religious chaos in Israel. By these measures, we can only conclude that he gave the Philistines a twenty-year nightmare.

And yet!

Hebrews 11:32–34 lists Samson alongside such saints as Abraham, Noah, Moses, and David and in the same cluster as the other judge-era leaders Gideon, Barak, and Jephthah. It says of such men that "although weak, their faith imparted power to make them strong! Faith sparked courage within them and they became mighty warriors in battle, pulling armies from another realm into battle array" (v. 34). Obviously, the inspirer of Scripture measured Samson's quality differently than we might.

Maybe we forget that the Lord measures righteousness differently. We look at the outward signs, but the Lord looks on the heart (1 Samuel 16:7). The apostle Paul explained this very clearly in Romans 4:5: "No one earns God's righteousness. It can only be transferred when we no longer rely on our own works, but believe in the one who powerfully declares the ungodly to be righteous in his eyes. It is faith that transfers God's righteousness into your account!" It is not honorable behavior that makes a person righteous; it is faith.

Teacher and author Jon Bloom imagines Samson's relatives musing about his faith as they retrieved his body from the rubble of Dagon's temple: "You can exercise faith while being unfaithful. Samson knew his strength came from God. He believed the angel's prophecy and he believed that God would bless his gift of strength when Samson needed it."[15]

Despite his obvious weaknesses, this seems to be Samson's subtle strength. We hear it when he cried out to God to quench his thirst. We hear it in his confession to Delilah. We hear it in his final prayer. He knew the Lord was the source of his strength and the one his whole life was dedicated to even before he was born. He knew that the Spirit was always the source of his power. He knew that if there was any victory, it came from the Lord.

In this, Samson's story began and ended with hope, hope for the rest of us. At times, we can be convinced that our failures and misbehavior have disqualified us from life in the Lord. We think that after we have burned through all of God's grace, he has lost patience with us. We conclude that we cannot be forgiven or restored this time. We believe that the sins that exhaust us have exhausted his mercy.

Then along comes Samson—this original avenger, who overcomes every enemy but himself—to remind us that righteousness comes only by faith. And if Samson can be in the household of faith, so can we.

 EXPERIENCE GOD'S HEART

- *Samson's moral compromises did not disqualify him from the benefits of faith, but they did come with serious consequences. The Christian cannot ignore the call to holiness. Make a list of some consequences you have faced because of your own sinful choices.*

- *Ultimately, Jesus bore the eternal consequences of judgment and death for anyone who will trust him. Reflect on the following verses to reinforce your understanding of righteousness through faith in Christ.*

  - Acts 13:38–39

  - Romans 1:16–17

  - Romans 3:20–24

  - Galatians 2:16, 21

  - Ephesians 2:8–10

♥ SHARE GOD'S HEART

- *When a believer shares their confidence in God, a common objection from skeptics arises. How can a good God permit such evil things to happen? Early in Samson's story, we learned that God could make use of human sin to accomplish his purposes (Judges 14:4). Jot down some thoughts about how this knowledge can help you talk about the Lord with others.*

- *Is a violent, carousing womanizer too far gone for the Lord? Samson wasn't. So, when your friend or relative believes they are too sinful to be forgiven, demonstrate the need for faith rather than the avoidance of it.*

Talking It Out

1. With your group, discuss the potential of reading the Old Testament with typology in mind. What new insights can we glean when we consider that many passages are pointing us toward Christ? Give some examples.

2. On the other hand, what danger is there in reading the Old Testament this way. How might we misunderstand a passage looking for an analogy to faith in Jesus?

3. Samson's mother dedicated him to the Lord as a Nazirite even before he was born. Discuss the burden of a lifetime as a spiritual example. Consider what might happen when others looked to Samson as a model. Can you understand why he might want out from under that heavy weight?

LESSON 9

Idol Hands

(Judges 17–18)

Most of the story in the Academy Award-winning 1994 film *Forrest Gump* centers on a man waiting at a bus stop. Not very captivating. Forrest's present wasn't the focus of the film though. His past—a whimsical, unpredictable odyssey—brought him to that moment on the cusp of transformation, so the film is largely a long series of flashbacks recounting that history.

Flashbacks give readers or viewers background information to help them understand the present narrative. The final five chapters of Judges are flashbacks to the early days of the Judges. The placement of the material is practical, not purposeful, but for the modern reader, it functions as a helpful flashback. It gives us great insight into the historical context of the judges and the desperate need for their leadership.

The book of Judges is a compilation of written accounts, researched and gathered to present a coherent history of the period between Israel's conquest of Canaan and the reigns of Israel's first kings. Obviously, no author was alive for the nearly five centuries covered in the narrative.

This anonymous compiler seems to have lived in a time when Israel was ruled by a king because four times in the final five chapters we read "in those days, Israel had no king" or a similar variation (Judges 17:6; 18:1; 19:1; 21:25). Early Jewish scholars believed that the prophet Samuel compiled this book, a project he may have pursued after anointing Saul and withdrawing from public leadership (1 Samuel 15:34–35). However, we cannot know the authorship for certain from the evidence we have in the Bible.

Having completed the history of Israel from Othniel to Samson, it appears that the compiler came upon two historical narratives from very early in the time of the judges. Pinpointing their precise moment in Israel's history remains difficult, though the text does have some helpful hints. Without access to a word processor, there was no way to cut-and-paste these narratives into the text at a more accurate point in the timeline, so they were simply added—handwritten—onto the end of the scroll.

After reading about deeply flawed judges like Gideon, Jephthah, and Samson, the reader might be tempted to question the wisdom of having such leaders at all. That is why these two episodes at the conclusion of Judges are so helpful. By YAHWEH'S divine guidance, they were placed at the end of the book to remind the reader of the spiritual and moral anarchy of Israel before these leaders. These accounts remind the readers of Israel's need for the judges. Furthermore, they stoke a longing for a better, more lasting kind of leadership for the people of God.

Confession Is Good for the Shrine

- *What crime did Micah confess to his mother (Judges 17:1–2)? Why do you think he confessed?*

- *What consequences did he face for his actions? Why?*

- *What awful product was made from the reclaimed silver (vv. 3–6)? In whose name was this wicked thing done? How was it incorporated into Micah's religious life?*

The first flashback establishes the rampant ethical and religious confusion of the era. Disrespectfully, a son stole a huge sum of silver from his own mother. Indulgently, his mother rewarded his confession of this crime with a blessing and a gift. Blasphemously, she dedicated the forging of a false god to the true God. Irreverently, this Jewish family set up a pagan shrine in their own home.

It's all so irrational and bewildering. How could people so patently blessed with divinely granted land, with startling material wealth, and with the rich spiritual heritage of the law of Moses be so confused about what is right? Why would they turn aside to idols and do it in the name of the Lord?

At Joshua's last address to the Israelites, he recognized their half-hearted commitment to the Lord. He predicted that they would not remain faithful to God's law, no matter how much they asserted their devotion.

Joshua warned the people, "Don't be so quick to say, 'We will worship and serve YAHWEH,' for he is a holy God. And he will tolerate no rivals. God will not forgive the sin of unfaithfulness to him. If after YAHWEH has been gracious to you, you turn away and forsake him to worship other gods, then he will turn and deal harshly with you and totally consume you!"

"No, no!" the people responded, "We promise to worship and serve YAHWEH!"

Then Joshua said to them, "You are witnesses against yourselves that you have chosen to serve YAHWEH."

"Yes, we are witnesses," they responded.

"Now then," said Joshua, "throw away these foreign gods that are among you, and yield your hearts fully to YAHWEH the God of Israel!"

And the people promised Joshua, "We really will worship and serve our God, YAHWEH, and listen to his voice." (Joshua 24:19–24)

Turns out, Joshua was right.

Priest for Hire

- *Describe the houseguest that Micah received (Judges 17:7–9). What was his tribe? Where was he from? Why was he traveling? Who was he (18:30)?*

- *What job did Micah offer this stranger (17:10–13)? What honorific title did he use for the Levite? Who held this position before him (see v. 5)?*

- *Why did this personnel change seem proper to Micah? What does he expect will result from this ordination?*

Unlike the members of other tribes, Levites had no land inheritance from YAHWEH.[16] Instead, cities were set aside in Israel for them. They received homes in those cities and farmland nearby. The fact that this Levite came from Bethlehem, a city not designated for the Levites, means that the Israelites were already dropping the ball on their obligation to provide for the tribe of Levi. The fact that he was available to take on a new job shows that the Levites were also dropping the ball on their religious obligations toward Israel.

Micah knew, however, that Levites were special. They were the family of priests and religious leaders. Since he had a Levite free agent there in his own home, he offered him the position previously held by his son. It was a position of honor and spiritual authority, and it came with a good wage, room, and board, so the Levite jumped at the opportunity.

Shopping for a Home

- *Who were Micah's next houseguests (18:1–2)? What was their mission?*

- *Why did the territory allotted to them after the conquest not work out for them (Joshua 19:40–48; Judges 1:34)?*

- *What old acquaintance did they find on their journey (Judges 18:3–6)? What did they ask him to do for them?*

- *At the end of their journey, what kind of community did they find (vv. 7–10)? Why was it vulnerable? Based on this reconnaissance, what action did the Danite scouts urge their tribe to take?*

Like the wandering Levite who was not where he was supposed to be and not doing what he was expected to do, along came the Danites. They also were not in their assigned territory fulfilling their calling.

Their land allotment lay to the south of Ephraim and west toward the Mediterranean. They were supposed to be claiming this land from the Amorites, fighting until they possessed it. But the Amorites "persisted in living" there (1:35) and were proving harder to subdue than the Danites expected. So they gave up and went in search of greener pastures.

The scouting party found a welcome and an old friend at Micah's place. They took note of the assets he had in his shrine. They also sought the advice of his priest for their undertaking. With his blessing they went on their way.

Far to the north, on the frontier of Israel, they found the city of Laish ripe for the taking. Isolated and peaceful, Laish was an easy mark, so the scouting party returned to convince the rest of their tribe to resettle there.

Raiding the Shrine

- *How big was the invasion force of the Danites (18:11–13)? Where did they revisit on their trek north? Why did they stop in there again (vv. 14–21)?*

- *What resistance did they encounter at the shrine? Why did the Levite cooperate?*

- *What was left for Micah?*

- *Who chased after the raiders to recover the looted property (vv. 22–26)? What was the effect of the confrontation? Compare this outcome to Micah's hopes in 17:13.*

Maybe because of his blessing on their successful mission to Laish, the Danites put their confidence in the Levite and his shrine idols. So with hundreds of armed men, they returned to Micah's shrine to plunder it. With all the idols gone, the Levite was out of a job. With the prospect of a more prominent role, he joined the raiders. Micah's ragtag local posse was no match for this company of warriors.

He lost it all. Micah expected to be blessed: blessed by his indulgent mom, blessed by the name of the Lord (taken in vain), blessed by his false gods, and blessed by his unfaithful priest. This idolater's confidence was grounded in lies, so all that he built was snatched away in one day. This thief was robbed, and his new false religion ensnared a whole tribe.

Founding "New Dan"

- *How successful was the Danite invasion of the new territory (18:27–29)? Why?*

- *What did this long narrative about Micah's shrine explain about the ongoing cultural and religious situation in northern Israel (vv. 29–31)?*

When they wiped out Laish, they renamed their new city after their ancestor, Dan the son of Israel. People commonly change the name of places they come to occupy. New Brunswick, New York City, New Hampshire, and New Zealand are just a handful of examples of places renamed by the new inhabitants for favored places in their past.

This whole move was unnecessary and harmful. God promised to enable Israel to take the entire land of Canaan. He would fight for them if they would stand with him. Like the other tribes, Dan could have had their promised land. By abandoning their inheritance, they destroyed a defenseless people who were not their enemies. Furthermore, they made it harder to belong to the people of God.

In this new region, among the Phoenicians, the Danites learned seafaring. By the time of Deborah, they "lingered near their ships" rather than answering Barak's call to fight their enemies with the other tribes (5:17). Moving so far north loosened their connection with the rest of Israel.

This move even splintered their own weak tribe. Not all the Danites migrated to New Dan. That is why the angel found Manoah and his wife, Samson's parents, living in Zorah among the remnant in the original territory assigned to the Danites (13:2). Samson's leadership was hindered by isolation from his own tribe and the domination of Philistines where Danites should have been.

Worst of all, their move made apostasy attractive. With a new priesthood and new idols, they were separated from the rest of Israel. Shiloh, and later Jerusalem, were far away. It was much easier to stay in their new territory and worship their new gods than travel all the distance back to participate in the worship of the true God. In fact, King Jeroboam makes this same argument when he sets up another idol in Dan more than four centuries later (1 Kings 12:26–30).

One more devastating consequence of the Danites abandoning their inheritance is evident in the last book of the Bible. When the Lord selects from every tribe twelve thousand faithful witnesses to be dedicated to him, one tribe is conspicuously absent (Revelation 7:1–8; 14:1–5). Dan is not even mentioned in this prophetic passage. They lost an eternal inheritance when they turned away from God's promise.

This was the chaotic environment in Israel during the period of the judges. They adopted and adapted the pagan worship they were supposed to supplant. The ethic of profit and power dominated. They abandoned God's assignments. Israel had the law of Moses, but even Moses' Levite grandson lived life as though it didn't exist. The Israelites needed new strong leadership. They needed the judges.

🌀 DIGGING DEEPER

After Joshua and the elders of his generation died, Israel plummeted into moral lawlessness. They had the law, but they routinely disobeyed it. If they had followed Moses' instruction to learn it and teach it to their children (Deuteronomy 11:16–21), the ignorance demonstrated in this Micah episode would have been impossible.

- *Name each specific prohibition from God's law. Then note where this law was violated in this episode and the reference.*

Law of Moses	Prohibited	Violated	Judges 17–18
Exodus 20:15			
Leviticus 19:4			
Deuteronomy 5:11			
Numbers 18:1–7			
Deuteronomy 12:8			
Numbers 35:2–3			
Numbers 33:51–54			
Deuteronomy 20:10–13			
Deuteronomy 12:11–14			

EXPERIENCE GOD'S HEART

The worship of idols can seem like a primitive problem for benighted people like the ancient Israelites, but there are plenty of idols around today. Think about the sacred objects, images, shrines, and holy sites where people still direct their religious devotion.

- *What attraction do images and statues still have for modern believers? Are these a part of your worship practices?*

- *Idolatry is a broader category than the worship of physical images. In the New Testament, for example, Paul explains that gearing one's life toward the accumulation of possessions is idolatry. An idol is anything we turn into a god, an ultimate, a center around which we orient our lives. It can be mental or metal, an ideology or an institution, a person or a passion. Whatever it is, it is something that is not God, but we regard it with such devotion that it becomes a god to us. Consider the following Scripture verses. Do they identify idolatry in your life?*

- "It has been made clear to you already that the kingdom of God cannot be accessed by anyone who is guilty of sexual sin, or who is impure or greedy—for greed is the essence of idolatry" (Ephesians 5:5).

- "Live as one who has died to every form of sexual sin and impurity. Live as one who has died to the desires for forbidden things, including the desire for wealth, which is the essence of idol worship. When you live in these vices you ignite the anger of God against these acts of disobedience" (Colossians 3:5–6).

💚 SHARE GOD'S HEART

- *Micah's family had a little true religion mixed in with their idolatry and error. In the absence of objective truth and faithful teaching, people latch on to any religious ideas that seem helpful. That is why you may know many people who hold on to some strange mix of religious beliefs about angels, reincarnation, candles, rote prayers, karma, Scripture, and superstitions. In the next spiritual conversation you have, ask questions about things like these. You might be surprised by the religious casserole they have consumed.*

- *With a proper priest installed, Micah was convinced that the Lord would bless him. That hope proved as false as his other gods. Sincerity does not make our beliefs true. Some of our friends or relatives are confidently putting their hopes in false beliefs. Pray for them.*

Talking It Out

1. Discuss why it is so dangerous for everyone to do what is right in their own eyes. How can people agree on what is right and wrong? How do we implement what is right and true? Can truth be enforced? Should it be?

2. The judges brought order to a chaotic era of anything goes. They were deeply flawed, but far better than nothing. We often complain about our political or spiritual leaders because they don't measure up to our ideals, but consider the horrors of having no leaders at all. As a group, thank the Lord for the leaders you currently have and pray for them like Paul tells us to (1 Timothy 2:1–4).

LESSON 10

We Need a King

(Judges 19–21)

The Bible is no sanitized book. Saints are also sinners. Heroes can also be villains. Biblical authors do not steer clear of gore, eroticism, treachery, or violence. They tell it like it is, even the upsetting parts. The final episode in Judges is upsetting, to say the least. The gritty violence, sexual bedlam, and fraternal warfare described there reveal a depraved, out-of-control culture without standards or moral leadership.

Before delving into the material of Judges 19–21, be warned: the material here is dark and disturbing. If it were made into a film, it would have to be rated NC-17.[17] If you are a young student of Judges, please find an adult to study this with you or pass over it altogether for now.

This final tale shows us that religious confusion and ignorance of the Law was not limited to Micah's household. A spiritually rudderless society always delivers licentious living and danger. In this case, it even led to civil war.

The Flashpoint in Gibeah

- *What kind of couple is at the heart of this story (Judges 19:1–4)?*

- *How were this couple estranged? What efforts were made to reconcile (vv. 4–10)?*

- *Why did the Levite press on to Gibeah instead of stopping over in Jebus (vv. 11–15)? What kind of welcome did they receive when they arrived?*

- *Who finally offered them lodging (vv. 16–21)? How did the Levite assure him that they would be no imposition?*

This story opens with a broken family. The Levite's concubine has abandoned him to return to her father's house. Remember, concubinage was a common institution, often owing to infertility or legal agreements. Whether the Levite has a legal wife as well we do not know. We do know that he wanted to reunite his household, so he went to get her.

On their return trip, they pressed on to Israelite territory expecting safety and a warm welcome. Instead, they were left in the street, a major breach of etiquette in the ancient Middle East. The only warmth shown to them was from an old man from a different tribe living among the Benjamites in Gibeah.

• *What did the locals demand when they interrupted their dinner (vv. 22–26)? How did the old man offer to protect his guests?*

• *What finally satisfied the locals? How did they treat the Levite's concubine?*

In the middle of dinner, local men banged on the door. They came on a vile mission. They demanded to have sexual relations with the traveling Levite. Hours before, these same townsfolk couldn't be bothered to shelter the stranger. Now they wanted to sexually assault him!

As host, the old man was obliged to provide safety to his guests, so he begged the harassers to stop. He even offered them his own unmarried daughter to satisfy their lust. Only when the Levite callously threw his concubine outside for them did they withdraw. They restrained her and spent the night raping her.

 DIGGING DEEPER

This wretched story from Israel in Canaan has an equally appalling counterpart from the era of the patriarchs. In Abraham's day, the two Canaanite cities notorious for the same kind of evil were Sodom and Gomorrah. Their infamy continues today as we still use the word *sodomize* to refer to their style of sexual abuse.

- *Compare the two accounts from Judges and Genesis and identify the parallel element found in Israel's Gibeah and the ancient twin cities that came under God's imminent fiery judgment.*

Sodom	Parallel Element	Gibeah
Genesis 19:1–2		Judges 19:15–20
Genesis 19:2–3		Judges 19:21
Genesis 19:4–5		Judges 19:22
Genesis 19:6–7		Judges 19:23
Genesis 19:8		Judges 19:24
Genesis 19:9		Judges 19:25
Genesis 19:24–25		Judges 20:48

- *What did the Levite find when he ventured outdoors in the morning (Judges 19:27–30)? What did he do with his lifeless concubine? How did his parcels affect the recipients?*

Indifferent toward the abuse his mistress suffered, the Levite demanded that she get up so they could travel home. She gave no answer, for she had no pulse. He didn't mourn. He didn't inform his host. He simply plopped her corpse on his donkey and took her home. Then he cut her up into twelve portions like a piece of meat and sent the grisly parcels to the leaders of Israel in every tribe.

Naturally, everyone was appalled. They convened an emergency national conference.

Outbreak of Civil War

- *What did the tribes discuss at their gathering in response to these ghastly parcels (20:1–11)? Which tribe was not invited?*

- *What details in the Levite's retelling differ from the narrative of the event?*

- *What did the tribes decide to do? Whom were they determined to punish (vv. 12–13)?*

- *How did the other Benjamites respond to the verdict (vv. 13–16)? Describe the numbers and skill of their forces.*

In their fury over Gibeah's treatment of the concubine, the Israelites made hurried plans and, as will become clear, uttered some impetuous oaths together. They determined that the tribe of Benjamin would surrender the villains who threatened the Levite and raped his concubine to death. These men would justly face the consequences for their brutal crime. Instead, Gibeah protected the rapists. The rest of the tribe of Benjamin, either from fraternal loyalty or pique from being snubbed in the national conference, stood with them too. So began Israel's first civil war.

• *What did the rest of Israel do about Benjamin's resistance (vv. 17–29)? How many times did they inquire of the Lord about the battle? Who was the high priest? How did their questions change in the process? Do you detect an attitude shift there?*

• *How did Israel finally defeat the Benjamites (vv. 30–48)? What excessive retaliation did they perpetrate in the aftermath of the battle?*

Confident that war was the right action, Israel inquired of the Lord who would lead the battle, not whether there should be one. Judah was appointed and then soundly defeated. Again, they inquired of Yahweh, but this time they asked whether they should fight. The result was another defeat. Tens of thousands were already dead.

When they inquired of the Lord one more time about the fight,

YAHWEH promised victory. In that battle, Benjamin was virtually wiped out with only six hundred men remaining. Their livestock were destroyed, and their cities were burned after their inhabitants were killed. The villains at Gibeah were finally punished, and that nameless Levite was avenged, but at a monstrous cost.

The nation was in tatters. Benjamin was holding on by a thread. Thriving innocent communities were reduced to smoldering ruins. But even in reconstruction, still more suffering lay ahead.

Reconstruction

- *What two rash vows did the men of Israel make at their initial gathering at Mizpah (21:1–7)? In conjunction with their excessive vengeance after the battle, what great problem did their oaths cause?*

Only as their tempers cooled did the rest of the Israelites realize the predicament for the nation. One whole tribe out of the twelve teetered on the edge of extinction. In their unconstrained bloodlust, they had wiped out the towns belonging to the Benjamites and their warriors. In fact, there remained no women or children to make a future for the tribe. On top of that, their unrestrained fervor against the Benjamites led to vows that they would never let their own daughters marry into this rogue tribe. No prospective brides remained in Israel. The last chapter is their convoluted attempt to solve this dilemma.

- *How did they address this problem (vv. 8–14)? Was it enough?*

- *What final strategy did they devise to help reconstruct the Benjamites (vv. 15–23)?*

First, they secured women through another massacre at Jabesh-Gilead. Its virgin daughters were taken as spoils of battle. These war brides grieved their families and community to solve Israel's self-inflicted predicament. Second, the mass abduction of hundreds of other women was necessary to complete the process. Only ludicrous ethical reasoning got them out from under their foolish vow. Only seared consciences could justify this kidnapping and the trauma it would cause these young ladies. The tribe of Benjamin was saved from annihilation but not without expanding their misery to others.

Morally, spiritually, culturally, Israel was a broken catastrophe of a nation. They were plainly incapable of governing themselves.

 DIGGING DEEPER

There's an old and reliable saying about the consequences of sin: "Sin will take you farther than you want to go. Sin will keep you longer than you want to stay. Sin will cost you more than you want to pay."

Tens of thousands dead. Settlements and communities obliterated. A fractured people. Grieving communities in every direction. Enormous suffering, but it all started on a smaller yet horrific scale. Israel's first civil war and its aftershocks were instigated by a carousing gang of perverts in the streets of Gibeah. Like a stone plunked into a pond, the effects went out from that moment to engulf a city, a tribe, and a nation.

- *Read through Judges 19–21 and identify each expansion of pain. Can you see any moments when humble repentance would have stopped the expansion? Note them below.*

Epilogue

- *What did Israel do after this dreadful civil war (21:24– 25)? What was the cultural foundation of all their spiritual and moral chaos?*

The battles were over. They had cobbled together something of a solution for Benjamin's survival. As each warrior turned toward home, they walked past fresh graves and wasted, ruined Israelite territory. All that was left was to return and carry on with their lives.

The way back was the way forward. Back to the land. Back to their starting point (Joshua 24:28). Back home. They could return to the promises of God. No matter how they behaved, they could count on him. Even when they were unfaithful, he remained faithful to his word. He brought them out of slavery. He made them a nation. He gave them their inheritance.

Regularly, we suffer the consequences of our selfish decisions, rash commitments, and rationalized sin. Our lives are always changed by these choices, of course. Others, too, are forced to deal with the consequences, participants and bystanders alike. Sometimes the wreckage is so complete that we wonder whether anything good can come of it. But like Israel, we pick up and start again, hopefully with some new awareness of our own intractable flaws and God's faithfulness.

The book of Judges closes with an oft-repeated theme. Having failed utterly to govern themselves, both individually and as a group, the Israelites needed some order. They would not survive if everyone only did what seemed right in their own eyes. They needed a leader who would direct them in a better way.

They had the law of Moses, divinely given at Mount Sinai. They had this written Scripture to orient their thinking, their lives, and their society to the will and character of God. They were aware of God's word while Moses and Joshua lived, but the slide came quickly (Judges 2:7). The final grim episodes in Judges mention grandsons of Moses (18:30) and Aaron (20:28), showing us that it took less than two generations to descend ethically from Sinai to Sodom.

Any society is vulnerable to this plummet into depravity. When objective truth is neglected or rejected, then right and wrong become personal opinions, and everyone does what is right in their own eyes. Shame diminishes, perversion is tolerated then celebrated, and secret immorality becomes public spectacle in streets and public spaces. Only widespread repentance and restoring righteousness to a place of honor can turn this trajectory. Only godly leadership can accomplish that.

Without a leader pointing the way, modeling the way, Israel quickly veered from God's revealed standard. Israel needed a king, a godly king, a God-King to lead them into the righteous life. Jesus the Messiah was the leader Israel needed. It would take them many generations to understand that. Only after their judges, their kings, their exile, and their religious leaders failed them would they be prepared for him.

They needed God's Messiah. We still do.

EXPERIENCE GOD'S HEART

- *For better or worse, society changes. Some behaviors and attitudes that used to be tolerated are now despised. Others that were once shameful are now tolerated and even commended. How have your personal ethics changed over time? How closely does your morality track with societal shifts? What standard do you use to evaluate right and wrong?*

- *Think of a time when your sin led to dreadful consequences. Sadly, this is easy for most of us to do. What pain did you experience as a result? How did you carry on afterward? Where did you find solace?*

♥ SHARE GOD'S HEART

- *Demonstrably, it was futile for the old man to challenge the men from Gibeah about their behavior. Sin had already made them callous. Could an earlier confrontation have helped? When do you think it is appropriate to confront evil behavior in others?*

- *How would you talk to a non-believer about sin? What attitudes should you have when you do?*

- *When our sin has harmed others, strong friendships can be broken. Resentments simmer. Bitterness poisons. Estrangement naturally, maybe inevitably, results. The alternative is reconciliation. Jesus taught that even our relationship with God is hindered when there is unresolved strife with others (Matthew 5:23–26). Making amends might be the best next step to carrying on with life. Even if your friend does not respond well, "Do your best to live as everybody's friend" (Romans 12:18).*

Talking It Out

1. Much moral compromise is individual, but groups also play their part. What can communities of believers do when society seems morally out of control? Make a list together of specific actions that Christians can take.

2. Judge-era Israel needed King Jesus, but it would be centuries until he was revealed. Today's world still needs him these many centuries after he appeared. Read four or five headlines of a newspaper with your group. Talk about how each situation would be different if King Jesus were leading us.

LESSON 11

Homecoming

(Ruth 1–2)

Wildflowers grow on the battlefield. Surrounded by the ugliness of violence, they stretch their beautiful petals toward the sunlight. In the reek of mayhem, they freely offer the grace of their fragrance to anyone who will stop to notice.

In chaotic times, ordinary life still offers its consolations. A refreshing landscape. A lover's embrace. A sound, dreamless sleep. A well-prepared meal. A sustaining friendship. The story of Ruth is one such wildflower of ordinary life sown "during the era when champion-deliverers ruled in Israel" (Ruth 1:1).

Since the judge who was ruling during this narrative goes unmentioned, we can only infer its date from hints in the text. The first passage shows us that Israel was in a peaceful relationship with Moab. The last passage indicates that it was only a few generations after slavery in Egypt.[18] From these hints, we infer that Ruth's life was likely contemporary with either Judge Othniel before Moab's oppression over Israel began or in the peace of Judge Ehud after Moab's defeat.

We can also infer that the book of Ruth was written many years later. The opening line presumes the days of the judges were past. The final passage gives us the names of generations beyond Ruth. As they do for the book of Judges, early Jewish scholars credit the prophet Samuel as the writer of the book of Ruth.

While the book is named for Ruth, it more closely follows the life story of her mother-in-law, Naomi. She is the subject of the first and last verses. Her sorrow, desperation, hope, and redemption through Ruth are the true focus of the story.

Leaving Home

• *What climate event led this family to move from Israel to Moab (Ruth 1:1–5)? List the family changes that happened while they were there. Who made up the household after ten years?*

Like Abraham, Isaac, Jacob, and Judah before him, Elimelech was forced to leave Canaan because of drought. His family of four crossed the Jordan to find food in the land of Moab. Almost immediately, the family was reduced to three.

Naomi's sons married local girls, Orpah and Ruth. Moses' law forbade Israelites from marrying Moabites (Deuteronomy 23:3–6), but Jewish women in Moab were as scarce as food in Israel. A decade into Naomi's Moabite migration, both her sons died, too, and the household was again down to three—Naomi and her two widowed daughters-in-law.

• *Why did Naomi head for home (Ruth 1:6–9)? When Naomi decided to return to Israel, what did she counsel her daughters-in-law to do? What blessings did she pronounce over them?*

• *What did the young women commit to do for Naomi? What reasons did Naomi give to dissuade them from their plan (vv. 10–18)?*

• *What did Orpah decide to do? What about Ruth? How thorough was Ruth's devotion to Naomi?*

When Naomi left Moab for home, she urged Ruth and Orpah to rejoin their birth families. When they refused to turn back, she insisted. What they needed more than a grieving old widow were virile young husbands who could provide for them and give them children of their own. Orpah, though obviously grieved by the parting, was persuaded by these facts. Ruth, however, would not turn back.

The language of blessing runs throughout this book. These wishes of goodwill in the Lord's name tell us a lot about the culture of those times, what was valued and what was not. Like our common goodbye (God-be-with-ye) and adios (to God) or a toast at a wedding reception, blessings were part of their daily and momentous interactions. Make special note of these blessings as you study this book.

Apart from 1 Corinthians 13, the New Testament love chapter, no passage of Scripture is more commonly read at Christian weddings than Ruth's profession of commitment to Naomi.[19] There was no place Naomi could go or stay where Ruth would not be. Ruth would leave her own people and religion behind to belong to Naomi. This was an until-death-do-us-part commitment before the Lord himself.

🔟 WORD WEALTH

These women were in desperate straits. There was no social security, no national pension plan for a widow. There were no IRAs or annuities to keep the monthly provisions flowing. Only the labor of their children could provide for them in their old age and disability.

One provision for these circumstances was the common practice of *levirate* marriage (Deuteronomy 25:5–10). The term comes from *levir*, the Latin word for brother-in-law. In this arrangement, when a woman was widowed, her husband's brother would take her as his wife. The first son produced from that union would be reckoned as the dead man's heir. The new son could receive the deceased man's inheritance. The dead brother's name would be preserved in history, and his widow would be provided for in her old age.

All three of these women were widows without children or the prospect of them. Naomi was too old for another marriage arrangement. Orpah and Ruth were young, but as Moabites, they were unlikely to find a husband in Israel. As foreigners, they would be more vulnerable to exploitation. Both brothers had died, so even *levirate* marriage was off the table.

Little wonder, then, that Orpah went home, and it was a great wonder that Ruth refused to.

Returning Emptyhanded

- *How did the community in Bethlehem react to Naomi's return (Ruth 1:19–22)? Why did she insist on using a new name? How do you think Ruth felt when she heard Naomi sum up her assets?*

When the women arrived in Bethlehem, the chatter around town was disbelief. They never thought Naomi would come home. Indeed, in some ways she agreed. The Naomi who left ten years before did not return. That woman had been pleasant, joyful, satisfied with her life and family. Instead, a bitter husk of a woman was all that remained of her. So she insisted they call her Marah now. Her perspective was clouded by grief and loss. Even with devoted Ruth standing there, she felt she had nothing.

A Field of Opportunity

- *What did Ruth do to provide for herself and Naomi (2:1–4)? Whose field was she working in? What was the landowner's connection to Naomi? How did Boaz greet his workers, and how did they respond? What kind of relationship do you sense there?*

- *Why was Boaz curious about Ruth's presence in his field (vv. 5–9)? How did the overseer describe Ruth's work habits? What additional kindness did Boaz offer Ruth?*

Without husbands or children, the widows had to rely on their own industry, so Ruth got to work. She found a nearby field at harvest and went about picking up the grain that the harvesters had dropped along the sides of the field.

THE BACKSTORY

No matter what economic system they use, every society has poor people. The Lord said as much (Deuteronomy 15:11; Matthew 26:11). When the Lord gave Moses his law to organize a new society around his character and principles, he did not forget about the poor.

- *Look up the following Torah passages and describe the provisions God made for the poor.*

The Lord's Protection or Provision for the Poor	Passage in the Torah
	Exodus 23:3, 6; Leviticus 19:15; Deuteronomy 24:14–15
	Exodus 30:15; Leviticus 14:21
	Leviticus 27:8; Deuteronomy 24:12
	Leviticus 25:25
	Leviticus 25:35; Deuteronomy 15:7, 11
	Exodus 23:11; Leviticus 19:10; 23:22

Primarily, provision for the poor was not in the form of hand-outs. Society expected the able-bodied poor to use their own hands to meet their own needs. So the Lord commanded harvest-ers to leave the edges of fields unharvested, to leave behind any produce they dropped, and never to gather second harvests. This left food in the fields and vineyards for anyone willing to work.

Such work kept the poor from taking advantage of the rich, and it offered every Israelite dignity. Only the truly disabled were dependent on their relatives for a living. This principle followed through into New Testament times when the apostle Paul wrote, "Anyone who does not want to work for a living should go hun-gry" (2 Thessalonians 3:10).

Ruth was willing to do the hard work of providing for Naomi and her own needs. Eventually, she would glean more than a day's food from this effort. The Lord was working to redeem them from their difficult circumstances.

- *How did Ruth's devotion to Naomi pave the way to favor with Boaz (Ruth 2:10–16)? What blessings did he pronounce over her?*

- *What public generosity did he show to Ruth? What secret generosity did he arrange for?*

- *What impressed Naomi when Ruth showed her the fruit of her work (vv. 17–23)?*

- *What did Naomi say about Boaz when she learned of his kindness toward Ruth? What unusual title did she use for him?*

Rather than repelling him, the fact of Ruth's foreign origin only seemed to draw Boaz. Knowing that she left her own family to remain a faithful daughter to Naomi impressed him. Boaz's own grandmother Rahab had been a Canaanite, after all. Her willingness to forsake her people to "find shelter" (v. 12) among the covenant people of God was part of Boaz's heritage. No other man could have appreciated Ruth's spiritual immigration more.

This man of good character was drawn to this woman of good character. Young people hoping to find someone to marry would be wise to take this to heart. While you are waiting, become the sort of person that the sort of person you want to be with would want to be with. Robert Watson observed that Boaz here "quickly and fully recognizes the goodness of another and will help her because they stand upon a common ground of conscience and duty...Character is known by character, and worth by worth."[20]

The compassion Ruth had toward Naomi moved Boaz to

compassion. Her sacrifice of kindness touched him, and he rewarded her with his own kindness. He gave her job security, protection, food, water, and a little extra besides. The biblical principle "to sow seeds of righteousness will bring a true and lasting reward" (Proverbs 11:18) was surely true in Ruth's case.

Her first wages were a welcome sight to empty Naomi. All the food they needed would be theirs. When she discovered who their benefactor was, she was overjoyed. She knew Boaz to be a good man who would ensure Ruth's safety. Besides, he was a close enough relative that he might be of even greater permanent help to them both. Naomi came home empty, but already, YAHWEH was literally filling her.

Loyal Ruth kept her promise. She went where Naomi went. She stayed where Naomi stayed. Now that Naomi was at home in Bethlehem, so was Ruth. Best of all, she was finding belonging with Naomi's people and her God. She was learning about the provision and kindness of both.

❤ EXPERIENCE GOD'S HEART

- *Have you faced a string of devastating losses like Naomi did? Did you feel the hollowness that she did? Can you remember the first consolations that reminded you that the Lord still cared about you? What people or events played a role in your first steps out of that pit?*

• *Has anyone ever shown faithful friendship to you? What would it mean to you if someone who could have walked away decided to stick with you? What kinds of practical differences would a friendship like that make in your life? How would that kind of devotion fill you up? If you have a friend like that, write a card to thank them.*

♥ SHARE GOD'S HEART

• *Think of some simple blessings you can offer others in daily life. Instead of the standard salutation on a letter, sign off with a wish like "courage" or "peace." When they drop by your house, say something like, "I hope your moments here fill you up." There are many moments that are begging for a blessing. It may sound silly or old-fashioned, but people are often pleasantly surprised when they are greeted in an offbeat way.*

- *When Naomi learned who had been so generous to Ruth, she recognized the goodness of* Yahweh. *Sometimes we need to share our experiences with people who are too numb or downcast to notice the Lord in their own lives. Do you know such a person? Along with praying for them, consider something from your own life that you could share that may lift their spirits.*

Talking It Out

1. In your group, talk about Deuteronomy 15:7–11. Could those principles work today? How does our society view poverty? Is it an illness to be cured with an infusion? Are the poor regarded as victims or free agents? Is poverty an obstacle to tackle with hard work and determination? Is it an institutional or individual problem? Is it about economics or ethics? What do you think?

2. Naomi left Bethlehem for ten years and came back changed. Thornton Wilder said, "You can't go home again." Has anyone in the group left their hometown or region? Have any of you returned after an extended time away? How did that sojourn in another place change you? Does home feel like home anymore? Why or why not?

LESSON 12

Redeemed

(Ruth 3–4)

When it comes to proposing marriage, most couples go for something meaningful and romantic. A walk on the beach or through the forest. A romantic carriage ride or dinner in a favorite fine restaurant. Because engagement is such a turning point in life, the couple will never forget the moment no matter how conventional the setting. But some suitors turn the memorability dial up to eleven.

Alexander Loucopoulos is a partner at a private equity firm focused on investments in water infrastructure. He's also a creative marriage proposer. In 2007, he booked a ninety-minute zero-gravity flight with his girlfriend so he could *float* the question.[21]

A man in IJsselstein, Netherlands, hired a crane to propose outside his girlfriend's high rise apartment window, but the crane crashed into the neighbor's apartment in the process.[22]

No matter how memorable these wedding proposals were, millions of Bible readers will remember how the question was popped in the book of Ruth. As much as Naomi loved that Ruth loved her, she wanted a different kind of love for Ruth, so she helped her plan an unusual wedding proposal.

- *What concern did Naomi always have for Ruth when she returned to Israel with her (Ruth 1:11–13; 3:1)? Who was she convinced could meet this need for Ruth (3:2–6)?*

- *What strategy did she give Ruth to follow? What did Ruth do to initiate the conversation with Boaz in the middle of the night (3:7–9)?*

Now that the harvest was over and the threshing done, it was time for winnowing the grain. The chaff had to be separated from the grain. To do this, grain was shaken in a basket or "cradle" until the useless dry husk separated from the healthy kernels. Then it was tossed into the air so the wind could carry away the lighter chaff and the remaining heavier grain would fall back down into the basket. This lengthy process occupied the workers late into the night and into the early morning, so they often slept on the threshing floor. Naomi knew that was where Ruth would find hard-working Boaz.

Making herself as attractive as she could, Ruth waited until Boaz fell asleep. Then she pulled the covers off his feet and lay down at the end of his bed. Some interpreters have suggested that this move was a sexual overture on the part of Ruth. It was bold enough and would have been understood as something intimate, but there is no cause to see seduction here. With cold feet, Boaz would likely stir in the night for the secret talk Ruth needed to initiate. The strategy worked.

- *How did Boaz respond to Ruth's proposal of marriage (vv. 10–18)? Why did he tell Ruth to leave before dawn? What parting gift did he give her to show her his favor? Why do you think Naomi believed Boaz would act quickly?*

When she asked Boaz to spread the corner of his garment over her, he understood immediately that Ruth was proposing marriage. The word for "corner of your garment" is often translated *wing*. In fact, it is the same word Boaz used to describe the Lord's refuge for her in 2:12. To spread his wing over her meant to become responsible for her life. Only one man could do this for a woman, namely, her husband. Following up her request, Ruth pointed out that Boaz was her kinsman-redeemer.

 # THE BACKSTORY

One of the provisions for the poor in Israel was the guarantee that, no matter how destitute a person might become, their land inheritance would not be sold away from the family (Leviticus 25:25–28). If financial difficulties were too great, a person could sell land, but close relatives had the responsibility to purchase it to keep the land in the family. The closest kin had the first obligation to help. He was the *kinsman-redeemer*.

In Naomi's case, her husband and sons had inherited property.

With all of them gone and Naomi in financial stress, the property was to be sold. Crucially, attached to the sale of Elimelech's land, though, was the familial obligation to care for his widow Naomi and widowed daughter-in-law Ruth. Redeeming the land meant redeeming the women too.

When Ruth called Boaz their kinsman-redeemer, she was asking him to take on all this responsibility: a piece of property, the old-age care of Naomi, and a levirate marriage to Ruth. Asking for redemption was asking for a wedding.

The offer did not overwhelm Boaz; he was honored and complimented. Ruth was younger than him. She could have set her affections on younger men. He admired and cared for her already, and he was only too happy to accept her proposal to marry.

However, there was one hindrance. Boaz was not the closest relative, and as a Hebrew of honor, he honored Hebrew custom. He needed to respect the other man's kinship rights. Boaz had a plan.

Nothing inappropriate happened between Boaz and Ruth that night, and to avoid giving the impression that it had, Boaz urged Ruth to leave before the other workers arose in the morning. He sent her home with a cloak-full of grain. Again, he wanted Ruth and once-empty Naomi to be filled.

Naomi sensed the hand of Yahweh in their relationship from the start. In his sovereignty, the Lord guided Ruth to the field of this eligible bachelor relative. He was wealthy enough to provide for them. He was closely related enough to redeem them. He could solve their entire dilemma. Now she knew that he would.

- *Where did Boaz go when Ruth returned to Naomi (Ruth 4:1–4)? Whom did he arrange to speak to about Ruth? Whom did he gather to witness their conversation?*

- *At first, what did Boaz indicate he was offering? Did the kinsman-redeemer want it?*

- *When the kinsman-redeemer learned that a widow was part of the deal, what did he decide (vv. 5–8)? What token did he give to seal the agreement? Who then redeemed Naomi's land and her widowed daughter-in-law Ruth?*

- *Why did Boaz make a show of this transaction (vv. 9–12)? What historical name and details did the elders mention in the blessings they pronounced over the engaged couple?*

Boaz recruited an audience for this dramatic negotiation in the city gate. In Israel, the gate of the city was where leaders gathered, issues were discussed, justice was done, and official business was transacted. An official transaction like the one Boaz had in mind would need to happen there in public with many witnesses.

Then he publicly explained to Naomi's closest relative Naomi's plan to sell Elimelech's parcel of land. Boaz urged the man to redeem that property since he was the closest relation. This seemed a done deal—until Boaz mentioned Ruth.

We do not know why the kinsman-redeemer balked at that moment. Was he already married? Was he concerned for his reputation? Was he unwilling to marry or father a child with a foreigner like Ruth? Did he realize that by producing an heir for his relative, he would eventually lose the property he would be redeeming? The text doesn't state his objection plainly, only that it would complicate his own estate. Somehow, to Boaz's delight, the man's mind flipped on the purchase.

They traded a sandal, signifying that the kinsman who did not redeem the property had no entitlement to walk there. They completed the transaction in front of elders and others as witnesses. And the townspeople pronounced generous blessings on the redemption and the marriage union to come.

- *What immediate blessing did the Lord give to Ruth and Boaz after their marriage (vv. 13–16)? What blessings did the women of the community shower on Naomi? What title did they use to describe Ruth's baby?*

- *Eventually, Ruth became the great-grandmother of what famous descendent (vv. 17–22)? What even greater offspring came through her lineage (Matthew 1:1–16)?*

 THE BACKSTORY

In the blessings, the elders pronounced over the redeemer Boaz and his family, we see how precious this small town was to the residents who lived there. At that point, Bethlehem already had a rich history and an even brighter future. The elders prayed that the couple would build up the family of Israel and that their descendants would be famous in Bethlehem. They had no idea!

When Jacob, the father of all the tribes of Israel, lived in Canaan, his beloved wife Rachel died giving birth to his youngest son, Benjamin. She died and was buried near a small settlement called Ephrath (Genesis 35:19), later known as Bethlehem. Both the town's names speak of abundance. *Ephrath* means "fertility," and *Bethlehem* means "house of bread."

This seemingly insignificant town in Judah was of greater importance as time went on. The book of Judges mentions Bethlehem several times, and the beautiful love story of Ruth occurs there. As the generations unfolded, three important people were born there.

First, Boaz and Ruth's first child, Obed, fulfilled so many hopes for the family. Naomi, who had lost everyone, now had a grandson who would look after her in her old age. Ruth's first husband had an heir so that his name would not be lost to history.

Ruth and Boaz could build on their love and grow their own family together.

Second, Ruth's great-grandson, King David, was born in Bethlehem. This shepherd king would rule from Hebron and Jerusalem, but Bethlehem remained close to his heart. On one occasion, when he was hiding in a cave, he wistfully longed for a drink from Bethlehem's fountain, and a few of his heroic men stole past their enemies to secure it for him (1 Chronicles 11:15–19). Bethlehem came to be known as the city of David.

Finally, another Shepherd Ruler was born in Bethlehem:

> "You, Bethlehem Ephrathah,
>   though you are small among the clans of Judah,
> out of you will come for me
>   one who will be ruler over Israel,
> whose origins are from of old,
>   from ancient times."
> Therefore Israel will be abandoned
>   until the time when she who is in labor bears a son,
> and the rest of his brothers return
>   to join the Israelites.
> He will stand and shepherd his flock
>   in the strength of the LORD,
>   in the majesty of the name of the LORD his God.
> And they will live securely, for then his greatness
>   will reach to the ends of the earth.
> And he will be our peace. (Micah 5:2–5 NIV)

This promise was fulfilled, of course, when Joseph hurried down to Bethlehem with Mary to pay his taxes in the town of David because he was from David's family (Luke 2:4–5). Soon after their arrival, the Messiah Jesus was born, and magi came searching for him in Jerusalem. Because of Micah's prophecy, Jewish leaders knew just where to find him. "He will be born in Bethlehem, in the land of Judah," they said (Matthew 2:5).

Redeemed!

Through God's sovereign guidance and steadfast love, Naomi and Ruth were redeemed. When we redeem something, we pay the price to rescue it. Boaz was willing to do that, so the whole family was saved. This redeemer from Bethlehem is the fore-shadow of Christ.

Every one of us is in desperate trouble. Our sin has us impov-erished and in bondage. We have no means to pay the price for our own freedom, let alone that of others. As the psalmist wrote:

> No one could give God the ransom price
> for the soul of another, let alone for himself.
> A soul's redemption is too costly and precious
> for anyone to pay with earthly wealth.
> The price to pay is never enough
> to purchase eternal life for even one,
> to keep them out of hell.
> (Psalm 49:6–9)

We need a redeemer. Thankfully, we have a Redeemer from Bethlehem, the Lord Jesus. He did not owe an unpayable debt. He was not in bondage to sin. He had not earned death, the just wage for sin (Romans 6:23). Jesus lived a life like ours but without sinning (Hebrews 4:15). So he was qualified to redeem us.

Our redemption was not a financial transaction. It was the substitution of the righteous for the guilty, Jesus' life for ours. He died the death we deserved, and now our Redeemer lives for-ever to offer eternal life to anyone who will believe. The saints in heaven declare it like this: "Your blood was the price paid to redeem us. You purchased us to bring us to God out of every tribe, language, people group, and nation" (Revelation 5:9).

If Naomi and Ruth were redeemed from poverty and despair, how much truer that is for those who put their faith in Christ. The Redeemer from Bethlehem is still redeeming people today.

 EXPERIENCE GOD'S HEART

- *It would be a tragedy to learn about Naomi, Ruth, and their redeemer Boaz without taking to heart this question: Are you redeemed? Have you recognized your total helplessness against the domination of sin? Have you put your faith in Jesus who died to pay your price? Has he bought you with his blood? (If these questions seem strange to you, look up the passages in the Talking It Out section below and pray that God will help you understand. Or better yet, ask someone who you are confident has faith in Christ to explain it to you. There is a Redeemer, and he paid the price for you.)*

- *If you do understand you are redeemed, say a simple prayer to the Lord. Thank him for paying the price for you. Thank him for substituting his righteous life for your sinful one. Thank him for loving you like that. Tell him that you are glad to belong to him. Tell him you want to live like a member of his family.*

❤ SHARE GOD'S HEART

- *In December, it is not uncommon to hear "O Little Town of Bethlehem" playing in public shopping centers. We seldom think of Bethlehem outside the Christmas season, but Christmas is a great time to talk to others about faith. Pique someone's interest with a question like, "Did you know that Jesus wasn't the only redeemer from Bethlehem?" or "Have you heard of the other babies born in Bethlehem?"*

- *Psalm 107:2 (NIV) reads, "Let the redeemed of the LORD tell their story—those he redeemed from the hand of the foe." If the Lord has redeemed you, you have a story to tell. How did you realize you needed a Redeemer? What turning points in your life led you to that? Who helped you understand? Where were you when you trusted Jesus as your Redeemer? Maybe telling your story will help others believe him too.*

Talking It Out

1. Share your wedding proposal stories. Talk about how costly
   or complicated engagements and wedding ceremonies
   can be. Why do we think this rite of passage is worth it?
   How far are we willing to go for that love? Does this tell us
   anything about God's thoughts toward us?

2. Look up the following passages together and talk about
   being redeemed: Psalm 130:7–8; Isaiah 59:20–21; Romans
   3:21–26; Ephesians 1:7; Colossians 1:13–14; 1 Peter 1:18–
   21. How did the Lord pay the price to rescue you?

❨

Endnotes

1   Brian Simmons et al., "A Note to Readers," *The Passion Translation: The New Testament with Psalms, Proverbs, and Song of Songs* (Savage, MN: BroadStreet Publishing Group, 2020), ix.

2   Suggested answers to the cycle: 1. Devotion; 2. Death of the leader(s); 3. Disobedience; 4. Discipline; 5. Distress; 6. Deliverance.

3   "From The Archives, 1975: *Edmund Fitzgerald* Sinks in Lake Superior," NBC News, November 10, 2020, YouTube video, 0:01:55, https://www.youtube.com/watch?v=z7tzntwy0_8.

4   Gordon Lightfoot, "Wreck of the *Edmund Fitzgerald*," track 2 on *Summertime Dream*, Reprise Records, 1976.

5   The gender of Junia is disputed but not widely so. Most scholars agree that she was called an apostle here, though not in the same sense as the Twelve were. The church father John Chrysostom wrote of her, "Oh how great is the devotion of this woman, that she should be even counted worthy of the appellation of apostle!" (Chrysostom, as quoted by John Temple Bristow, *What Paul Said about Women: An Apostle's Liberating Views on Equality in Marriage, Leadership, and More* [San Francisco, CA: HarperSanFrancisco, 1988], 57.)

6   Ellen Hendriksen, "Failure to Launch Syndrome," *Scientific American*, May 18, 2019, https://www.scientificamerican.com/article/failure-to-launch-syndrome/. Many of the articles about this phenomenon are based on research done prior to the COVID-19 worldwide disruptions. Most indications point to an increase of this syndrome in the aftermath.

7   Barry G. Webb, *Judges and Ruth: God in Chaos* (Wheaton, IL: Crossway, 2015), 136.

8   Ian Thomas, "The U.S. Army Is Struggling to Find the Recruits It Needs to Win the Fight over the Future," CNBC, October 26, 2022, https://www.cnbc.com/2022/10/26/us-army-struggles-to-find-recruits-its-needs-to-win-fight-of-future.html.

9   Theodore Camp, "The Military Depends on Virtues That Are Fading," *Public Discourse*, March 24, 2023, https://www.thepublicdiscourse.com/2023/03/88095.

10 If you would like to do a biblical study of the origin and initial consequences of human sin, we suggest the Bible study guide *TPT: The Book of Genesis*, parts one and two (Savage, MN: BroadStreet Publishing Group, 2022).

11 Michael Card, "Why?," track 6 on *Known by the Scars,* Sparrow Records, 1989.

12 See Gleason L. Archer, *A Survey of Old Testament Introduction*, rev. ed. (Chicago, IL: Moody Press, 2007), 256.

13   These aspects of Samson's life are fulfilled in Jesus: His own people rejected him (John 1:10–11), cooperated with their oppressors to have him killed (18:28–32), and delivered him, tied up, to foreign enemies (Matthew 27:1–2). Through the righteous wrath of God, at the final battle, Jesus will finally supernaturally defeat all his foes in a total triumph (Revelation 19:11–21).

14   For example, see Webb, *Judges and Ruth*, 212.

15   Jon Bloom, "The Weakness of the World's Strongest Man," Desiring God, January 17, 2014, https://www.desiringgod.org/articles/the-weakness-of-the-worlds-strongest-man.

16   "The Lord gave the Levites special responsibilities and privileges. They were allowed to be closer to his holy presence than any others. Theirs was the priesthood, including the high priesthood. They offered the sacrifices. They could handle the ark of the covenant. They ministered in the tabernacle and tended its furnishings. These privileges granted them the honor and respect of the rest of the Israelites. In all these promises of an intangible inheritance, God also made provision for their practical needs. They were allowed to eat from the offerings the rest of their countrymen made at the altar (Numbers 18:8–10; Deuteronomy 18:1–5). The Israelites were to give a tithe, a tenth, of their wealth, toward providing for the Levites (Numbers 18:20–24; Deuteronomy 14:22–29). Finally, the Israelites would provide the Levites with towns to live in and the pasturelands around those towns for their livestock (Numbers 35:2–5)." *TPT: The Book of Joshua: 12-Lesson Study Guide* (Savage, MN: BroadStreet Publishing Group, 2024), 175–76.

17 The "Classification and Rating Rules" of the Motion Picture Association state, "An NC-17 rating can be based on violence, sex, aberrational behavior, drug abuse or any other element that most parents would consider too strong and therefore off-limits for viewing by their children" (Motion Picture Association, "Classification and Rating Rules," July 24, 2020, sec. 3, para. C [5], https://www.filmratings.com/Content/Downloads/rating_rules.pdf). This last episode in Judges clearly qualifies for such a rating.

18 Ram was born a Hebrew slave in Egypt, and his children were certainly born there. His grandson Nahshon was in the generation who survived the wilderness wanderings and marched around Jericho. Matthew's genealogy tells us that Nahshon's son Salmon married Rahab, the faith-filled Canaanite of that city (Matthew 1:5), and fathered Boaz. Boaz was Rahab's son and some years older than Ruth (Ruth 3:10).

19 Incidentally, neither of these common wedding passages are about Christian marriage. One is the exhortation to self-giving love that holds the body of Christ together in unity. The other is a profession of a child's undying devotion to a parent.

20 Robert A. Watson, *The Expositor's Bible: Judges and Ruth*, ed. W. Robertson Nicoll (New York: Funk & Wagnalls, 1900), 393, https://ccel.org/ccel/watson_ra/expositor7/expositor7.v.iii.html#v.iii-p1.2.

21 Kelly Tracer, "Out-of-this-World Marriage Proposal," *Greeley Tribune*, May 13, 2020, https://www.greeleytribune.com/2007/05/07/out-of-this-world-marriage-proposal.

22 "Dutch Marriage Proposal Sees Crane Smash IJsselstein House," BBC, December 13, 2014, https://www.bbc.com/news/world-europe-30462825.